# Working-Class Fiction in Theory and Practice
## A Reading of Alan Sillitoe

# Working-Class Fiction in Theory and Practice
## A Reading of Alan Sillitoe

by
Peter Hitchcock

U·M·I Research Press

Ann Arbor / London

Produced and distributed by
UMI Research Press
an imprint of
University Microfilms Inc.
Ann Arbor, Michigan 48106


Library of Congress Cataloging in Publication Data

**Hitchcock, Peter.**
  Working-class fiction in theory and practice : a reading of Alan
Sillitoe / by Peter Hitchcock.
    p. cm.—(Challenging the literary canon)
    Bibliography: p.
    Includes index.
    ISBN 0-8357-1976-6 (alk. paper)
    1. Sillitoe, Alan—Criticism and interpretation—. 2. Labor and
laboring classes in literature. I. Title. II. Series.
PR6037.I55Z75   1989
823'.914—dc19                                                        89-4747
                                                                          CIP

British Library CIP data is available.

*to my mother, to my father, to my brother*

# Contents

# Acknowledgments

I would like to thank the patient staffs of both the Graduate Center Library of the City University of New York and the New York Public Library for their help. I would also like to thank my friends and relatives in England for helping me to gather the necessary research materials. There are many other people who have helped to write this book in ways they might not know. Perhaps one day we will "write" some history together. Finally, I extend my gratitude to Morris Dickstein for developing this project. His encouragement has not gone unnoticed, although any errors of judgment that remain are all mine.

# Introduction

*There can be no language (except a dead one) without speakers. . . . Language is continually fought over in its words, syntax and discursive deployments.*

—Richard Johnson

In Alan Sillitoe's most famous short story, "The Loneliness of the Long Distance Runner," the main character, Smith, wonders whether anyone will get the opportunity to read the story he has written about how he deliberately lost the running race for the Borstal in which he was imprisoned. It is a literary sleight of hand of course, because there are the words before us, but the only reader that Smith mentions is the governor of the Borstal, Smith's tormentor and enemy: "I'd like to see the governor's face when he reads it, if he does, which I don't suppose he will; even if he did read it though I don't think he'd know what it was all about."[1] Smith has good reason to doubt whether the governor will read his story not just because to read or not to read is a reader's prerogative, but because from a theoretical perspective the governor simply cannot read the story that Smith has told. It is not a question of eyes scanning the page but more the obverse of that much maligned term "cultural literacy"; obverse in that it is often the case that those forces, symbolized to a degree by the governor, that constitute a cultural hegemony in any given society are those which usually "govern" what is held to be readable and what is not. For Smith, however, "cultural literacy" is being able to read and understand him, a position that for some may seem untenable but is nevertheless implied in the pages that follow.

This book is not about Smith, nor, perhaps surprisingly, is it "about" his inventor Alan Sillitoe—at least not in the accepted sense of the one author/one corpus critical approach. It is, rather, an attempt to analyze and explicate the cultural forces at work in the production and reception of a literature that challenges and to some extent undermines predominant notions of the literary. Why Sillitoe is crucial to this study is because his works, indeed his literary career, throw into stark relief the theoretical and sociopolitical problems involved in assessing what we may call the counter-literary. Specifically, the counter-literary is here held to be working-class writing and, although the hallmarks of this form of expression cannot be reduced to the body of Sillitoe's work, the latter nevertheless provides some important guidelines and lessons that need to be addressed.

The argument in this study proceeds on three interdependent levels: the historical, the textual, and the formal. The first chapter tracks working-class fiction in an English context in order to historically situate Sillitoe's contribution within a broader scope of cultural production. That there are limitations to an approach that eyes the components of one national culture is clearly evident, but it does allow a perspective on the specific development of these components. The problem of deducing any general principles from this is addressed later in the book. The key period in Sillitoe's writing career is 1958–61, years in which his work was celebrated as the flowering of a new literary talent. I will argue that this "discovery" can only be adequately interpreted by understanding the cultural dynamics of the late 1950s and early 1960s, a moment in cultural history that is analyzed under the general rubric of the "cultural event." It is the workings of the cultural event that allow us to trace not only the rise to prominence of Alan Sillitoe, but also his speedy marginalization in the British literary scene.

The core of this study utilizes textual and formal analyses, which may be seen as a departure from the sociological inclinations of the early chapters, but in fact builds upon the conceptual framework that these provide. The cornerstone of the approach is an adaptation or mutation of Bakhtin's theory of dialogism, which allows a language-based exegesis of Sillitoe's writing as "working class" without falling back on content-oriented methodologies. As I hope to show, the multiple voicing of working-class fiction represents not only its most salient aesthetic quality, but also its specific internal polemic. Again, it is this aspect of, for instance, Smith's literacy, that makes the governors of this world wince.

Although the idea of working-class fiction is not new, its low currency within contemporary critical debates might suggest to some that interest in such work is only reserved for those content to dig one more literary artifact from the burial ground of history. We live in a period of the postmodern and the poststructural, a time when class is bracketed and any claims to subjectivity are placed under erasure or sometimes convenient provisionality. This is not the place to mount some rearguard defense against such claims, particularly since they are often positively implicated in the study that follows. Nor would it be adequate to simply dismiss such tendencies as "neo-conservative" or ahistorical, even when in the practice of some critics this is quite clearly the case. The reason class is important to these debates is because they are about political struggle, and they are most assuredly about questions of history. History is what hurts, as Frederic Jameson has reminded us, and perhaps that is what makes theorizing working-class fiction a painful process, even more than justifying the truth claims of Smith.

What is working-class fiction? In one respect this is a false question like Sartre's "What is literature?" because it presupposes that working-class literature *is*. If class subjectivities are themselves under theoretical question then theorizing the possibilities of class-based literature would seem a thankless task, but nevertheless one might brush the present, if not history, against the grain by making some initial (and by all means provisional!) distinctions. Working-class fiction is writing by working-class writers; proletarian fiction, however, can be considered the work of class-conscious members of that social stratum with a particular class-specific political program. Socialist fiction too displays a political commitment, this time as a product of writers who may well be other than working class. Such crude distinctions do not make working-class fiction apolitical, but suggest its political aims are not simply a reflection of class destiny or consciousness. To theorize such writing requires an approach that goes beyond reflectionist theories of class content, and also avoids a heavy reliance on suspect models of authorial intentionality.

In a well-known essay in *Some Versions of Pastoral*, William Empson develops a notion of proletarian literature by simply omitting the question of class altogether.[2] His "definition" that good proletarian art is "usually Covert Pastoral" is not without substance, particularly with regard to the cultural scene of the 1930s that he surveys. Since Empson's approach has previously been challenged in direct relation to Sillitoe, I will do no more here than comment on the implications of what has been a very influential method of pigeonholing working-class fiction.[3] Empson's argument steadfastly attempts to separate his aesthetic rendering of class-based literature from any consideration of politics or economics because these apparently "do not provide an aesthetic theory." What he is after are the more "permanent ideas" embodied in such fiction, archetypes if you like, that do not bow to the more immediate concerns of the political sphere. There seems little point, however, in talking of proletarian literature at all if one denies precisely those dimensions in which "proletarian" makes any significant sense. Thus, while Empson's essay is rightly lauded for the seriousness of his concern, his broad critical brush strokes effectively obliterate historical understanding of the subject at hand. Nevertheless, there are moments in the essay when Empson gestures in the opposite direction. At one point he states that "literature is a social process, and also an attempt to reconcile the conflicts of an individual in whom those of society will be mirrored."[4] What is provocative here is not the reflectionism invoked, but the inference that reconciliation itself may be part of the literary process. For contemporary theorists, the idea that literature may be an imaginary resolution of the real contradictions of a society at any one moment of history is not an alien concept, and suggests that literature may indeed provide the reconciliation that Empson wrote about some fifty years ago.

Many critics on the Left have pursued the question of "imaginary relations" in the space that links literature and ideology, but relatively few have attempted to do this in relation to working-class writing.[5] Within the academies of Western Europe and North America there is a certain political, if not cultural, logic to this situation, but fortunately there are signs that that logic is now under question, even as it remains the dominant one of our time. In this sense, we may read the relative neglect of working-class writing as a symptom of the political constituency of the university as an institution of knowledge, or cultural literacy. It is also, however, indicative of a more general crisis of theories of representation which have made questions of class and culture difficult to articulate.

For Alan Sillitoe questions of class and culture, particularly those concerning the idea of working-class fiction, are held in deep suspicion. On one level this reflects his general distrust of all labels, but also perhaps a perfectly understandable reaction to a critical formulation that has usually meant the kiss of death to a writer trying to catch the eye of the literary establishment. Sillitoe's belief in the working class itself has generally been consistent and even in his recent fiction, for instance *Down from the Hill,* working-class life continues to be a major focus of his writing. In response to Sillitoe's rejection of critical labels, David Craig has suggested, following D. H. Lawrence's maxim, that we trust the tale rather than the artist. With this I concur, but I hope in the proceeding pages my mistrust is read as productive and not simply as a dismissal of Sillitoe's authorial predilections. Sillitoe's voice should still be heard in these pages, as should others, particularly those of Mikhail Bakhtin and Raymond Williams, whose work in the analysis of language and culture has spurred my desire to come to terms with the problematic presented by "working-class fiction." Perhaps more questions will be asked than answered regarding this subject, but better to ask than to remain in silent complicity.

# 1

# In the Tracks of Working-Class Fiction

In *The Making of the English Working Class,* E. P. Thompson suggests that "The working class did not rise like the sun at an appointed time. It was present at its own making."[1] The cornerstone of his belief rests in the notion of *agency:* The working class was not just the result of productive relations, it was an agent of its own making. It is a point that Thompson has returned to consistently throughout his career, and nowhere more forcefully than in *The Poverty of Theory*—a book that almost single-handedly buried the excesses of Althusserianism in English Marxist theory.[2] There, in a generally vociferous attack on Althusser's theory of historical process without a subject, Thompson goes on to explain that "classes arise because men and women, in determinative productive relations, identify their antagonistic interests, and come to struggle, to think and to value in class ways: thus the process of class formation is a process of self-making, although under conditions which are 'given.'"[3] Although I do not wish to be drawn into this particularly stormy debate (which has been sufficiently discussed elsewhere),[4] it should be clear from what follows that I do not see the problem as simply being a choice between Althusserianism and non-Althusserianism, especially regarding theories of ideological determinations. I am interested, however, in further analysis of the concept of working-class agency, because it seems to me that if we cannot theorize the process of class formation, then any consideration of cultural production specific to class is bound to seem the most abstract and idealist of exercises. If indeed, the works by Sillitoe that I will discuss later constitute a working-class cultural intervention, then we must attempt to understand the complex relations that render such an "act" meaningful.

For Thompson, at least, these relations are viewed within a broadly humanist framework. "Agency," to this degree, allows history to be writ large by human activity—a belief that also fires Thompson's predilections for the role of "experience" in the formation of class consciousness. I do not have as many qualms about this formulation as Perry Anderson has in his critique of Thompson;[5] nevertheless, class agency is not quite the self-making that

Thompson would have us believe. Class, in Marxist terms, is an objective social relation: people become working class by their objective position in a system of relations of production. The spirit of this formulation indeed finds itself in Thompson's work, and few would attempt to deny it. Yet it is clear that the objective position described by Marx is established irrespective of particular attitudes, or what Thompson calls the ability to "think and value in class ways."[6] The importance of the Marxian thesis that "social being determines conscious-ness" is that it calls attention to the role of economic structure in the determina-tion of human subjectivity. Such a formulation does not deny agency, but defines the relations in which class agency becomes possible. Although Thompson has shifted his position since 1963, the role given to agency in *The Making of the English Working Class* has colored to a degree much of the historical research in this area.[7] Indeed, it is characteristic of the broader "cultu-ralist" trend that I trace in the next chapter. Yet the question remains whether any simple restatement of the primacy of the economic is enough to explain the processes inscribed in class-specific cultural production. If the cultural is secon-dary to the economic, then the relationship between the two is disjunctive rather than sequential. Any theory that attempts to smooth this relationship is determin-istic in the vulgar sense. The point is not to discount Thompson's use of agency in relation to culture, but to radically theorize it.

What I will attempt to do in this chapter is map one strand of working-class culture—its fiction—in order to lay something of the historical groundwork for the period study that appears in the next chapter. Two points are at issue here: the first is to explain why the English working-class writers of the 1950s, of whom Alan Sillitoe is clearly a major representative, lacked a recognizable tradition on which their work could build; and concomitantly, I want to analyze whether there is any validity to the claim that working-class writing only fully emerges in times of social crisis. Both points are linked through the question of agency that Thompson's work initiates, and both are intended to provide some kind of historical prologomena to my focus on Alan Sillitoe. Walter Benjamin begins his essay on Nikolai Leskov by noting: "Familiar though his name may be to us, the storyteller in his living immediacy is by no means a present force. He has already become something remote from us and something that is getting even more distant."[8] For Benjamin this was a sign that the great art of storytelling was coming to an end. But if I hold a similar view with regard to Sillitoe it is to reinscribe a historical perspective of the author as producer, and to suggest that there is yet one art of storytelling that has hardly been "born."

As Gustav Klaus is quick to point out in his book *The Literature of Labour,* there have never been many working-class writers in working-class cultural history. In the face of this relative scarcity what gives Klaus's "literature of labour" its solidity as a body of work is the inclusion of non-working-class writers and sympathizers. Here the issue of agency is clearly integral to Klaus's methodology. Klaus maintains that the "literature of labour" cannot "leave out the massive contribution of writers not born into the working class, but bringing a seriousness of concern, an acceptance of the subjectivity of the working class and of its objective role in the historical process, to their presentation of proletarian themes."[9] The advantage of this approach is that Klaus can trace working-class subjectivity in fiction even if the working class itself were not the agent of its production. The disadvantage of this approach lies in its advantage. In what way can the specificity of working-class fiction be addressed if it is not written by the working class? The plea here is not for a separatism based on the purity of authentic working-class writing, but rather for a tactical orientation of what Pierre Zima has called *les cultures subalternes*.[10] For instance, the reason male writers are not included in Elaine Showalter's *A Literature of Their Own* is not because it is impossible for men to write profeminist fiction or indeed not just an analytical convenience, but because establishing a counter-tradition requires principles of difference as a preliminary guide to selection. Subsequently, camp followers may well be considered, but their initial exclusion is a political imperative. Similarly, a critical focus on *working-class* writers of working-class fiction might at least allow some theoretical perspective on their governing characteristics. It is better that the literature of labor be barely "literature" than for it to be barely labor.[11]

The critical power of Klaus's book lies not in the process of selection employed so much as the historical method he applies to the works discussed. Indeed, this makes his contribution more significant for our purposes than the survey approach of Phyllis Mary Ashraf's extensive research on this subject.[12] For instance, by carefully considering the social determinants of eighteenth-century English society, Klaus shows convincingly how plebeian poets consciously attempted to give written expression to the oral traditions of their culture. They faced many obstacles, including limited access to formal education, few if any publishing outlets, and regional as well as class snobbery. The reasons why a number of these poets, including Robert Tatersal (bricklayer) and Mary Collier (clothes washer), received public recognition produce some interesting lessons for the period study I provide in the following chapter.

Part of the recognition was based on the fact that the middle and upper classes were simply amused and charmed by lower order attempts at the "literary." Yet sympathetic scholars were less condescending in their desire to see the "plebeians" get into print. Often they would track down prospective buyers for the workers' literary production and, through subscription, obtain the necessary financial guarantees for the publisher.[13] In mid-twentieth-century England a large, literate, and consumer-oriented working class would guarantee that advance subscription would not be necessary for production costs to be met. Yet several parallels can be stressed. First, Stephen Duck in the eighteenth century, like Alan Sillitoe in the twentieth, had access to, but not control of, the means of literary production, reproduction, and distribution. Second, their work would be subject to similar though not identical criteria of literary "taste," the ideological mediations of cultural hegemony. Third, their literary expression is bound by a dependence on received, or traditional, literary forms. The literature of labor can in neither case be considered autonomous or specific in purely formal terms. All of these points have theoretical implications for the last chapter of this book. Here, however, let me suggest that many of these conditions obtain for any literary production. But when social subject positions are considered across the full range of class stratification, including the sphere of ideology, the productive constraints of the writer are indeed overdetermined by class:

> Each new class which puts itself in the place of one ruling before it, is compelled, merely in order to carry through its aim, to represent its interests as the common interests of all the members of society, that is expressed in ideal form: it has to give its ideas the form of universality, and represent them as the only rational, universally valid ones.[14]

Literature, of course, is not a mere reflection of this universalization, but neither is its development entirely divorced from it. One comes to realize that literary opportunity is not created equal, and even when members of the working class do break into the literary sphere, their writing is precisely mediated by alien concepts of what constitutes the literary. Yet here again we must address the question of agency.

An alternative thesis to Thompson's concept of agency, where the working class has substantially made itself by 1832, is that the working class is continually the agent of its own *remaking* at any one moment in history, a recent reassessment of historical process notable in British historiography.[15] This does not mean that the working class necessarily transforms the mode of production, for such an act is contingent rather than inevitable. The working class changes the way it defines itself against the capitalist mode of production. In this sense, agency is not an act that has easily definable boundaries. Certainly, Thompson's meticulous history shows that *a* working class was made in the forty years he discusses, but there is more than a mild sense of essentialism to the claim that this is *the* English working class. Furthermore, even if we hold to the thesis of incessant class redefinition we must say that the agency involved is a particularly determined volition, considered within a historically specific economic structure. In this light class identity is the site of conflicting social forces: agency itself is riven by class struggle.

Class agency may well have cultural expression, but I will continue to insist throughout this work that class struggle and cultural struggle are not synonymous, and that their relationship is historically uneven rather than simultaneous. What this means for reading working-class fiction is that we cannot view the history of such cultural expression as an ontological reality, as the essential cultural markers of continuing working class "existence." To do so would be to construct a seamless tradition to which such work can rarely aspire. Instead, working-class fiction defines itself by its nontraditional status; indeed, by its antitraditional discontinuities. The history of working-class fiction is marked by disruption not only because working-class culture is oppositional, but because bourgeois cultural hegemony cannot allow it any other role.

What are the salient features of these disruptions or cultural interventions? One thesis, popularized by P. J. Keating in his book *The Working Classes in Victorian Fiction,* is that it is "only during moments of social crisis that any significant number of English novelists have attempted to write fiction centred upon working-class life."[16] There is some credibility to this contention, and much of the rest of this chapter will attempt to analyze its implications. Given, however, what has been said in relation to agency and tradition, the logic of Keating's version of this thesis is particularly illuminating:

> In so far as it is possible to talk at all of a genuine working-class literary tradition in the Victorian age, it is to be found in certain regional poets (both dialect and non-dialect), in a considerable mass of Chartist verse and doggerel, and most interestingly in the memoirs of working men who rose to positions of eminence in public life. Apart from a few Chartist novels imaginative prose is non-existent. A critical search in Victorian literature for a working-class tradition leads inevitably to the pessimistic conclusion reached by William Empson: "It is hard for an Englishman to talk definitely about proletarian art, because in England it has never been a genre with settled principles, and such as there is of it, that I have seen, is bad."
>
> Theoretically, of course, it is not necessary to be of the working class to write an outstanding novel about the working class. . . .[17]

First, Keating identifies what he believes to be the closest approximation to a "genuine working-class literary tradition in the Victorian age"; then goes on to note that "imaginative prose" is almost nonexistent within it. One must, of course, ask who is attempting to construct a tradition here (the chapter itself is called "The Two Traditions, 1820–80")? Keating continues by noting that a "critical search" (presumably his own) for a working-class tradition leads him to Empson's conclusion and, significantly, to non-working-class writers. It is the latter who thus come to produce Keating's own tradition and they are the same writers who respond in fiction to the social crises of the nineteenth century. My point is not to dismiss Keating's argument but to underline how tradition-building in literary studies, bound as it often is by bourgeois aesthetics, by itself is unable to account for the sporadic cultural incursions of the working-class writer. Tradition-building using working-class fiction can often lead to the construction of a cultural lacuna that petty bourgeois writers (particularly in the nineteenth century) are brought in to smooth over. In effect, Empson's "pessimism" is our most useful pointer here, for it is precisely the lack of "settled principles" that defines oppositional culture (and not just "bad" art). Working-class writers must make their marks by any means necessary. As for novelistic production during social crisis, there is much to Keating's claim, as long as it is not taken as some absolute law of literary expression. Here I want to consider whether the principle only holds good for middle-class writers, or whether in fact working-class writers made a significant contribution. The two crises that demand most attention for our purposes are the moment of Chartism in the 1840s and the Depression era of the late 1920s and 1930s.

Keating is not alone in stressing the importance of the period of Chartism. Martha Vicinus has provided the most detailed account of working-class writing during this crisis.[18] Chartism was a political movement charged with the desire to transform English society into a democracy that respected worker power. And political activism also had cultural expression:

> Culturally Chartist writers sought to create a class-based literature, expressive of the hopes and fears of the people. The years of the movement saw an outpouring of speeches, essays, prison letters, dialogues, short stories, novels, songs, lyrical poems, epics and, later in the century, autobiographies. As with so many political movements, the richest literary period came when the movement was declining and its political goals seemed more remote than ever. Most Chartist fiction dates from after 1848.[19]

Here, the fictional representation takes on many expressive forms, but the important point is that Vicinus believes that the major Chartist fictional representations develop on the coattails of the political movement. This is not some contemplative lag but, as Vicinus suggests, it is a problem of form. The governing characteristics of Thomas Martin Wheeler's *Sunshine and Shadow* (1849–50) and Ernest Jones's *De Brassier: A Democratic Romance* (1850–51) are precisely the manifestation of such technical difficulties. What is the fictional form appropriate to the class analysis of the movement?

> The lack of appropriate literary models had led both Wheeler and Jones to adapt the popular novel of the day. This had provided useful conventions and had touched a familiar chord in readers by means of the melodramatic style and characterization, but the form was too rigid and innately conservative to be effective for the heavy weight of politics imposed by the Chartists.[20]

Like the plebeian poets before them, Chartist writers find themselves in a position where they are the agents of their class-specific consciousness, but not the literary forms in which that solidarity is promoted. Nevertheless, the importance of this intervention is never underestimated. Wheeler points out that "the opponents of our principles have been allowed to wield the power of the imagination over the youth of our party, without any effort on our part to occupy this wide and fruitful plain."[21] There is no doubt that for the Chartists cultural production was necessarily a political project, but one where it was difficult to fuse culture and politics without one seeming to intrude upon the other. Within the fiction, for instance, political statements appeared to detract from the literary conventions with widest popular appeal. In addition, the conventions themselves limited the political import of each tale. In Jones's *De Brassier*, melodrama is useful for underlining the ruling class chicanery that may thwart democratic purposes but unfortunately, as Vicinus points out, it also highlights passive virtues in the working class which, even if they did form an objective characteristic of the class, are hardly likely to bolster a sense of historical agency. In any event, most of the political effectiveness of Chartist fiction is not achieved through the publication of individual works but by the juxtaposition of different political discourses within one and the same work. Thus, although the formal constraints of melodrama may prove insurmountable in their own terms, the serialization of such stories within Chartist newspapers and journals gives the works an "utterance context" (a term that will be fully explained in the light of my own textual analysis)[22] that draws the fiction into reader relations that suggest much more than passivity. This is evident in some of the editorial statements of Chartist newspapers like this one from *The Labourer:* "We, however, had one great goal before our eyes—the redemption of the Working classes from their thraldom—and to this object we have made the purpose of each article subservient. . . . We have placed poetry and romance side by side with politics and history."[23] The contradictions posed by individual fictions do not disappear in their newspaper form, but other discourses that accompany them underline that the problems of these particular aesthetic effects are not necessarily endemic to the political discourses of the movement as a whole. Ultimately, the important point is that the political fiction of the time struggles against formal elements that appear to compromise either the effectiveness of the fiction, or the impact of the politics.

The uneven development of artistic forms in relation to the political discourse of working-class radicalism gives further support to the idea that content is always in search of an appropriate form. In the England of the 1840s it *seemed* that a political crisis would produce the revolutionary content ripe for a revolutionary form. Yet Chartism was defeated and, one could argue, the opportunity to produce working-class forms was lost. Roland Barthes, looking at the failure of the revolution in France in 1848, suggests that a crisis in bourgeois ideology precipitated a sharp self-criticism on the part of the bourgeoisie—at the level of the literary this meant a burgeoning interest in stylization as an answer to the fact that the universal bourgeois subject was a little less than universal—"his conscience no longer corresponded precisely to his condition."[24] Barthes suggests that from that point on bourgeois writers became more experimental while socialist or communist writers stepped into the boots that they had left behind.

The crisis in England produces very different literary effects although they are not without correlative implications. For Chartist writers imbued with a sense of political destiny the populist approach guaranteed a similar readership to that of the penny journals at the same time as it cheapened the quality of writing. The stories often reflected the fascination of working-class readers with the machinations of the upper classes, but this generally excluded detailed narration of the working class as *subject*. The argument here is not against the fascinations of the working classes, but the exclusion of their subjectivity. This is as true of the work of Wheeler and Jones as it is of the "most popular writer of the time," G. W. M. Reynolds, whose consistent support for the poor still did not persuade him that the working class could be represented except as a group of generally debased and corrupt individuals. Part of the political crisis that is the moment of Chartism is, I would suggest, a crisis of representation. It would be wrong, however, to infer that this crisis was primarily a working-class problem in producing working-class writing. Indeed, few of the Chartist writers with any notoriety were of working-class origin—Jones, for instance, came from a wealthy family and, although his political activism on behalf of the working class was unflagging, he never experienced the "lived relations" of that class firsthand, and remained at some distance from it throughout his career. Thomas Martin Wheeler was a notable exception: a baker by trade, his fiction, particularly *Sunshine and Shadow,* has come to be the litmus paper of worker writing in most of the literary criticism of Chartism (including that of Vicinus, Mitchell, and Klaus).[25] Like Jones, Wheeler provides a historical overview of Chartism from a position where the movement has already been defeated. Unlike Jones, he sees the root of this defeat as a problem of leadership. Apart from differences in content, however, Wheeler's fiction seems bound by the same limitations as his middle-class comrades. Perhaps, in event, the historical consciousness that these writers encouraged is, as Klaus contends, their most notable contribution. In this respect the work of Chartist writers forms an interesting contrast to that of middle-class writers outside the movement, the work of the so-called industrial or social-problem novelists—Dickens, Gaskell, and Disraeli.

There is little space here to discuss their contributions in detail, yet it is quite clear that for them a crisis of representation proceeds from a very different ideological problematic. There is no need to recount that during the period under discussion there is a quite successful bourgeois fiction, fiction in which the specifically bourgeois ideologies of self-making and self-help (the Samuel Smiles syndrome) are offered up as the image of a class in dominance. Yet, as Raymond Williams has pointed out, these works in no way represent the sum of middle-class fictional production; indeed, the middle class was rarely their chief audience.[26] What Williams calls the "deep forms" are where I take the complexities of bourgeois ideology to be contested and worked as fictional representation. The industrial novelists, like their Chartist counterparts, are not unaffected by class consciousness but their political "unconscious" is driven by

(1) a view that their modes of representation are "emergent" and (2) that this emergence is dependent upon the subordination of alternative or competing representations. The working classes do not appear in their fiction as the product of some philanthropic urge (although this cannot totally be denied): they *must* be represented, or face the consequences of leaving the space for such cultural representation to those most aptly equipped to fill it. Thus, Dickens's *Dombey and Son* is both an exposé of the horrors of industrialism and a veritable denial of the working class ability to fundamentally alter such a state of affairs. Williams's comments on the importance of the subjunctive in chapter 47 underline Dickens's awareness of social possibilities, but one must add that Dickens precisely represses those "possibilities" that would call his own class position into question. Williams would disagree that the appearance of the working class in the fiction of the middle class is an ideological negotiation of class antagonism, although his own argument admits that class reconciliation is not absent from the "deep form."[27] What he emphasizes is "the significant openness of certain of the new impulses; of the inclusion of certain realities of the class situation and of class conflict; the pushing through to certain intensities however difficult they then were."[28] True, part of the major significance of the industrial novels of the time is their openness and that they do not fall back on the simplistic aesthetic "solutions" of explicit ideological production (for instance, the idea prevalent in many popular magazines that the solution to personal poverty was will power and sobriety). Yet here surely we have a parallel with the writers that Barthes mentions; their "openness" is itself conditioned by a similar sense of crisis, they must "push through to certain intensities" or admit the failure of their social vision, their "way of seeing." Thus, although their literary solutions to ideological contradictions are not homogenous and are hardly bourgeois in the obvious sense of class production, they nevertheless provide (according to an Althusserian conception of ideology) imaginary solutions to the real contradictions of their existence. Furthermore, the class effects of their production constitute the most successful literary works precisely *because* the management of contradictions resides deep in the form. In the case of Dickens, the tension between the traditions of community existence and the progress represented by the railway in *Dombey and Son* effectively substitute for the class antagonism lurking beneath the surface in the "dealings of the firm." What then are the lessons of the working-class fiction of this period?

If Chartist fiction failed to capture the imagination of the working class as Wheeler hoped it would, this is not directly analogous with the failure of the movement as a whole: the cultural production itself cannot, or should not, be made to seem a simple mediation of the political character of the Chartist movement. Indeed, it is quite possible to track the development of working-class representation without Chartism as a springboard—for instance, in penny fiction that does not subscribe to a Chartist position. Nevertheless, the limitations of the Chartist novel, as a representative of a more or less subordinated culture, that is, a culture that takes the representation of the working class as an integral mark of opposition, go a long way to explaining why the incursions of working-class fiction are so sporadic. It is not that we need a model of social crisis to highlight the appearance of this fiction but an understanding of class and cultural formation at any one moment of history. The discontinuities of working-class writing are not to be found in the history of social crises in which the working class is a significant factor; they are rather to be traced in the complex interactions of class and culture that may or may not depend on particular moments of social disjunction. Just as the political unconscious of the industrial novelists responds to historical developments beyond the immediacy of the Chartist experience, so too must the authors of Chartist fiction for, as we have seen, their particular problems of literary production are not symptomatic of the movement as a whole. Such an approach not only helps to explain why the working classes are a subject of fiction before becoming an author of it, but also why, when workers do in fact become authors, they do not necessarily overcome the problems of the "silence" or marginalization of their culture as a whole. The fact that *Household Words* is often taken as a major cultural representation of the working class, whereas *The Literature of Working Men* (whose contributors were all laborers and tradespeople) is not, cannot simply be reversed by an insistence on working-class agency as the prerequisite for working-class effects—but neither can we hold to a view which assumes that the established legitimacy of Dickens and Gaskell necessarily precludes a reevaluation of their "authority." To this extent Keating's work, while sympathetic, fails to understand the cultural struggle at stake in the representation of the working class.

Bruce Robbins's recent contribution, *The Servant's Hand*, is an important argument for the destabilizing influence of the representation of servants in English fiction and has considerable relevance to our discussion. Robbins shows that in much of the Western literary tradition the working class has an effective presence in texts as a curious appendage: the servant who, particularly in nineteenth-century bourgeois fiction, appears as the member of the underclass the writers know best since many of these writers indeed had servants. As a displacement for actually knowing the working class, the servant functions in particularly contradictory ways within individual texts. Among other points, Robbins proves that we can move beyond Orwell's conception that "if you look for the working classes in fiction, especially English fiction, all you find is a hole."[29] The working class is there, but not in the form we expect. This, of course, is only part of the story. As I have suggested, to adequately trace working-class writing one must have the working-class writing (the working class as writers). Politically, there is no point in filling a hole by digging another. There are other important theoretical implications to Robbins's book that I will address later but here it should be stressed that as our theoretical understanding of class and culture readjusts to current political imperatives, cultural critics often turn to the rewriting of cultural history. The fact remains that there are cultural histories that are as yet unwritten.

There is a further interpretation of the history of Chartism that is worth considering, if only to help map a critical model for working-class writing. Gareth Stedman-Jones's *Languages of Class* is a book about English working-class history that stands traditional class analysis on its head. Thus, he begins:

> In order to rewrite the political history of the "working class" or "working classes," we should start from the other end of the chain. Language disrupts any simple notion of the determination of consciousness by social being because it is itself part of social being. We cannot therefore decode political language to reach a primal and material expression of interest since it is the discursive structure of political language which conceives and defines interest in the first place.[30]

By applying a nonreferential conception of language, Stedman-Jones is able to work loose the "naturalized" correlation between the political discourses of Chartism and the English working class. That is, he shows that much of the political rhetoric of the period is a development of a burgeoning radicalism that is not specific to the working class. In this sense the Six Point Charter is not commensurate with the "objective aims" of the working class but is the renewed discursive formation of a radical tradition. This, of course, would be another way of explaining the uneven development of the working class in relation to working-class writing and helps to untangle the complicated knot of agency and class consciousness that we witness during this period. But even though it will become clear that my own emphasis is language-based, class is not quite the discursive reality that Stedman-Jones would have it. The reason many historians have taken Chartism to be a working-class movement is not on the basis of a few selections from Chartist speeches (which seems to form the core of Stedman-Jones's historical method), but through an exhaustive and sometimes exhausting recovery of documentation of various forms. As our own comments have shown above, the interrelationship of utterance with context helps to define the governing characteristics of the movement. Such work does not occlude the radical tradition of which Stedman-Jones writes, but shows how this political discourse is put to use and transformed by a different, historically specific context: an approach that guards against forms of abstract subjectivism that may come to obscure any objective relations of historical process. Thus, although we cannot say that there is no expressive relationship between language and class, class may be more than a discursive formation.

The value of Stedman-Jones's approach is not to be found in the reconstruction of history through discursivity, but in the arguments he makes for political discourse and constituency. For instance, we can see that in the political rhetoric of Chartists like O'Brien, McDouall, or Leach, the working class is indeed interpellated as an agent of political action: their constituency is addressed as part of the movement's broader aims. This effect powers the working-class fiction of the time, although it is compromised to a degree by the exigencies of available literary traditions. Ultimately, the importance of such conjunctions cannot be simply grasped by a nonreferential view of language; only in the realm of the referent can we avoid the fraught equation of "the ideological effect equals the aesthetic effect" despite the fact that both are nevertheless active components of the working-class effects of working-class fiction. Such a realization casts the following comments by J. M. Rignall in a much more productive light:

> The Chartist novelists seem to have left no direct heirs, for in the years between the demise of Chartism and the re-emergence of socialism in the 1880s there are no novels with the political vigour of Wheeler's *Sunshine and Shadow* and Jones's *De Brassier*. What little fiction there is by working-class writers tends to have gained in literary sophistication and imaginative grasp of the reality of working-class life, but at the expense of political awareness and socio-critical ambition.[31]

Again we have the suggestion that without crisis or a strong workers' movement, working-class fiction founders in relative quietude. Rignall, however, also provides a more plausible explanation in the same quotation. Working-class writers improve their abilities in conveying a sense of the social situation of their class without providing much political understanding of the broader implications of that situation. Aesthetically this problem is compounded by a more general acceptance of the "conventions of the respectable bourgeois novel" (e.g., including elements such as a mismarriage, overspending, debt, disaster, and reconciliation). Where the authors of the "deep form" interrogate the formal constraints of the novel, working-class novelists in particular accommodate these limitations. Although this is not a recipe for despair, it is certainly one for mediocrity, and contributes to a series of relatively anonymous production throughout much of the second half of the nineteenth century. I do not intend to attempt a history of those years (indeed, Rignall provides some exceptions to this otherwise grim picture, suggesting that further analysis would have to be predicated on precisely such a history), but it seems to me that in a society where working-class expression was looked upon with suspicion, any challenge on the terrain of *the* Victorian bourgeois cultural form, the novel, would have taken an artistic acumen and determination far in excess of the attempts that have so far been recorded. Perhaps the enormity of that challenge itself was overpowering. Perhaps, as Williams points out, like working-class writing outside the novel, the working class itself was still seeking to find a social voice adequate to its social force.

All through the nineteenth century, there were working-class writers. Only they were rarely writing novels. Verse of several kinds, and some vigorous work-songs. In prose, pamphlets, memoirs, autobiographies. That is either writing in the direct service of the cause, or writing as a record of it. Or, as in the increasingly popular form of the autobiography, of which hundreds of examples are still being recovered, the story of a man who had served the cause, or had become important through the cause, or who had "risen" from the class to some other eminence. A mixed history, but the accessible form individual, even when middle-class fiction was already, in its own terms, social.[32]

The history of this period could well be tracked through working-class fiction, but it continues to be partial because of the particular restrictive possibilities of an alien set of cultural codes. I will return to this point in relation to the Angries, but here it should be noted that certain forms of habitus are, by definition, exclusionary in terms of cultural capital.[33] Only by a consideration of a shared code, language, can we surmise how these world views collide.

Before providing analysis of the 1950s and 1960s that combines both an articulation of cultural formation with a closer look at the implications of language as cultural capital, more than passing mention should be made of the moment that beyond all others suggests that working-class fiction is indeed primarily a product of social crisis: the Depression era from the General Strike of 1926 to the Second World War. Since this period is often seen as the seedbed for the Angry production of the fifties and sixties, one should note at the outset that few of the later writers like Sillitoe were directly influenced by the *writing* of this period so much as they were by actually experiencing the deprivations of the time firsthand. Nevertheless, there can be no doubt that this particular "literature of crisis" forms the most extensive collection of committed fiction in the history of working-class writing in Britain.[34] This period sees significant contributions by Lewis Grassic Gibbon, Walter Brierley, Walter Greenwood, and Harold Heslop. Why? Most accounts fall into line in ways typical of Ramon Lopez Ortega's description:

> The Depression was at once the fuse that fired and the cement that bound these writers together. The spectre of unemployment and industrial conflict haunts the pages of their work; it lurks behind all the recurrent images–poverty, the fruitless search for work, life on the dole, the Means Test, the hunger marches, the strikes. These events conditioned the writers' perspective and, ultimately, their literary consciousness. Thus, whatever may have been their specific political convictions, they all attempted to enlist the sympathy of their readers, striving for solidarity with the working class.[35]

Few would deny that Lopez Ortega's comments elicit some social understanding of the nature of literary production, if we can accept that social being determines consciousness. The problem is whether consciousness of social situation is the precondition to literary agency. Why should this be important? If class-specific writing is *only* the product of class consciousness then the dynamism of such terms is lost: we simply have to match literature with the consciousness of which it is a supposed expression. This is quite possible, but I believe we should also entertain the notion that cultural production itself can mediate *between* social being and consciousness rather than being just an effect of the latter. In this sense, we can account for literary agency that proceeds in spite of conscious identification, or literature that consciously denies that identification only to reinscribe such links at the level of the unconscious. One model of analysis here does not cancel out the other; it rather suggests that both are necessary for tracking the shifting sands of working-class fiction, with or without significant social crisis. In this way we can follow literature that is both the effect of consciousness and that which in some sense produces consciousness.

Lopez Ortega's account of working-class writing of the thirties is particularly interesting because it is a language-based critique. In example after example he shows that the working-class specificity of this writing is not necessarily bound by party predilections or what is usually written off as tendentiousness, but by the particular language-use juxtaposed in individual texts. Apart from the intentionalist overtones, Lopez Ortega's approach yields some insightful observations, like these on Henry Green:

> While successfully mining the resources of working-class and current idiom, he was equally aware of the strengths of earlier English literary forms. The result is a terse, energetic and elliptical prose which, as Edward Stokes (Green's major critic) observes, is "essentially the industrial workers' style." The linguistic economy of *Living* certainly catches the factory atmosphere and the ethos of the working community. But this statement requires clarification: it does not mean that Green's almost telegraphic prose literally mirrors the sparseness characteristic of a proletarian environment. His artifice in my opinion is far more subtle: a consistent use of parataxis and asyndeton allows the fundamental facts of working-class life to stand out more clearly. As I see it, his solid style well translates the main features of the restricted code usually employed in working-class communication.[36]

Language style is a mediation rather than a mirror of working-class life. The linguistic economy of which Lopez Ortega writes begins to distinguish working-class writing not just on the basis of content, but on the way that content is communicated. This is surely different from the writing of the Chartist period, much of which hoped that content would make up for the inadequacies of form. Here writers like Green, and, particularly, Gibbon in *A Scots Quair* take language as the means of their art, language style as critique rather than reflection. In this sense, the significant working-class writers of the thirties were not exploiting the legacy of Chartist fiction, but the "deep form" of the Victorian industrial novelists. What was emergent in the fiction of Dickens and Gaskell, however, was residual in the works of Greenwood or Brierley, and may explain why working-class realism walked in the shadow of modernism until the Second World War.

As for the use of restricted codes (a term borrowed from the work of Basil Bernstein),[37] this had been evident in working-class fiction since the phonetic approximations of Tressell in *The Ragged Trousered Philanthropists* and D. H. Lawrence in *Sons and Lovers.* Lawrence, of course, is a particularly interesting case because he represents a working-class writer who struggled to overcome the restrictive inheritance of the nineteenth century. What is extremely ambiguous in his work, including *Lady Chatterley's Lover,* is whether his formal innovations are the product or a rejection of the class purview of his youth. Whatever Lawrence's ideological misgivings were, Morel and Mellors appear to have "survived" them. Few critical works thus far, however, have engaged in a thorough investigation of this ideological dilemma.[38]

Tressell's contribution remains the most enigmatic, partly, I believe, because of the ineffectivity of the "crisis" model in which he is more or less shuffled. Although Tressell was clearly aware of works by Gissing, Morrison, and Besant before writing *The Ragged Trousered Philanthropists,* his novel did not become inscribed in the debate that their work fostered. Tressell (Robert Noonan) died in 1911 and *The Ragged Trousered Philanthropists* was posthumously published in an abridged form in 1914. Its literary life in working-class culture did not begin until the twenties, when it was adapted for the stage by Tom Thomas for the Hackney People's Players. Thereafter, as Peter Miles has pointed out, it became distinguished by the diverse ways it was disseminated. It was not only a book to read and pass on, but an "active" component of class struggle—for instance, two hundred copies were once sold at a building site in Putney where a strike was in progress. *The Ragged Trousered Philanthropists* is a perfect book for such contexts because it makes reading habits of this kind part of its storyline and contains didactic speeches that have particular resonance in situations of class antagonism. These may not constitute an "overt" crisis so much as the ongoing and differentiated struggles wrought in the relations of labor and capital. Thus, although Tressell's book was popularized in the Depression years, it has continually appeared in other situations where class interests may seem to be at stake. Miles records how one copy was passed among English troops in Burma until it "literally fell to pieces."[39] Alan Sillitoe was first given a copy while he served as a radio operator in Malaya, and was told that it was the book that won the 1945 election for Labour. In 1955 an unabridged edition was published for the first time and from 1965 this edition has been available as a mass market paperback with, significantly, an introduction by Sillitoe. We will see that even though working-class writing does not constitute a tradition, patterns of influence and forms of dissemination are clearly operative, but suggest that relations of cultural production may or *may not* develop with broadly defined social upheaval. Certainly, although Tressell had a working-class readership in mind, its working-class effects have been most significant at specific moments even Tressell could not have predicted (for instance, a recent TV production of the book "reads" very differently against the background of Thatcher's Britain). Some understanding of the cultural relations of production and distribution at any one moment of history would throw into relief particular inscriptions and reinscriptions of working-class writing. This, indeed, is the rationale for a "reading" of Alan Sillitoe.

Three points should be reiterated at this stage. The first is that when considering the historical development of class-specific fiction, we should not assume that any class effects can only accrue in times of economic or social crisis. Class culture and class politics are not synonymous despite their intimate interrelationship; therefore, a theory of working-class fiction must account for those moments when culture and crisis do not coincide. Second, I have stressed the role of agency in literary production in order to clarify the notion of the "working-class" as cultural producers. This may indeed have the effect of separating the work of sympathetic bourgeois writers and the writing of committed socialists from that of the working class, but this separation is by no means absolute—which is reflected in my use of the term "class effects" (proclass cultural activity that may be the work of producers outside the class they support). Finally, writing in the tracks of working-class fiction requires an understanding of the social construction of working-class writing as a marginal cultural activity: a recognition that necessarily entails ideological analysis of both the production and reception of culture at any one moment of history. That class analysis undermines the isolation and explication of individual authors within such an approach is not meant to make their individuality disappear; indeed, this is precisely the reason why I focus on Alan Sillitoe regarding textual exegesis. Nevertheless, ultimately historicizing working-class fiction means attempting to explain how the class orientations of writing are always more than the individual intentions of this writer or that. To "read" in this way is thus to reassert that people do make history, but not alone or under conditions all of their own making. The following chapters are articulations of the above historicity.

# 2

# The Cultural Event

In his introduction to the collection *Society and Literature, 1945–70*, Alan Sinfield observes that "the cultural identification afforded by literature depends upon the mediation of literary forms and cultural institutions."[1] It is an interesting point, and one that could be culled from many a critic aware of the crucial concerns of contemporary theory. What is particularly noticeable is that the groundwork for such criticism was developed precisely in the period that I wish to discuss in this chapter. That is, the theoretical paradigm that allows us to understand the mediation of working-class fiction in the late 1950s and early 1960s in England has its inception at that moment in cultural history when such fiction had apparently burst upon the scene. Obviously, one has to take great care in asserting the significance of this conjunction, for one risks falling back on a prior vulgar reflectionism that theories of mediation themselves wish to displace. Nevertheless, the methodologies employed to trace particular moments of cultural production in the previous chapter are the product of theoretical developments made since the fifties. In this light, the appearance of some sixty working-class novels inside a decade plus numerous plays and of course the multitude of films with working-class themes makes this period singular and provocative. For what may seem a crisis of representation (i.e., how do you render the subjectivity of the working class meaningful when that subjectivity is itself in crisis?) is also, and more emphatically, a crisis of theoretical apprehension. What a period study can show are the parameters of this crisis and the workings of culture and society in which Alan Sillitoe's writing becomes manifest. It thus, in no small way, reveals the relations of cultural production and reception that too often leave working-class writing, like feminist fiction, "hidden from history."[2]

To map what I will develop as the "cultural event," one must have some sense of the historical forces at work in this conjunction, a consideration that must begin with the situation of the postwar English working class. It does not take a great deal to see that after the Second World War "the gravediggers of capitalism" in England, like their American and Western European counterparts, became relatively much better off than they had been before the war, and in comparison to so-called Second and Third World proletarian social formations. But it is also equally true that this perceived "affluence" tends to obscure the new changes and constituents of the English working class. Just as the Depression helped to clearly differentiate the "haves" from the "have-nots," an experience through which Sillitoe's own "us and them" consciousness was formed, so the gains in standards of living fired by the availability of jobs and the expansion of the international economy drastically complicate notions of class identity and identification. The dynamics of capitalism, particularly late capitalism, require a dynamic apprehension of working-class constituency. Those ideologues who blithely contended that the working class had simply disappeared, and with it the necessity for understanding ideology as Daniel Bell would have it,[3] were clearly dependent on older models of class analysis whose historical determinants history itself had called into question. The structural changes in the working class are not simply reflected in the material under discussion, working-class literary expression is part of the process of class reconstruction: they are dialectically bound up in the same objective relations of class determination. Sillitoe's *Saturday Night and Sunday Morning* should not be read as an effect of class change; rather, it is a cultural component of that change.

Although the English working class in the fifties was as heterogenous as the class in formation that E. P. Thompson describes, several factors were radically altering its composition. Many of the traditional working-class occupations—mining, shipworking, steel making—began to be undermined by foreign competition, notably American, but also by the resurgence of the German and Japanese postwar economies. In addition, the growth of multinational companies now found the English working class occupying a very different position from its prewar character. In a period of high employment levels and stable or rising relative wage levels, workers were recast not just as those who subsisted by the sale of their labor, but as a group with significant purchasing power. In a word, more than ever before, the English working class became defined and interpellated as *consumers*. If the logic of capitalism had previously sought to "naturalize" the extraction of surplus value from the *labor* of the masses, now it attempted to guarantee that any surplus wages were absorbed in the act of consumption. The productivist ideology of the early twentieth century ameliorated worker alienation with its concomitant political agitation by, among other developments, promoting the idea that work itself was a fulfillment. By mid-century the contradictions of this ideology were glossed by a further consumerist ideology which purported to guarantee self-worth in the possession of things. To be sure, an articulation of the roots of these capitalist relations can be found in Marx;[4] what should be noted, however, is that these theoretical suppositions had not been realized on such a scale before in practice. If car workers in England were surprised by the fact that even as workers they could now afford to buy cars, Leftist theorists despaired at what this meant for the working class as revolutionary historical agents. Part of the Leftist confusion is understandable. How could the collectivity be mustered for revolutionary transformation when "affluence" seemed to be producing an "I'm all right, Jack" individualism?

Yet the working class itself was not affluent across the full range of its employment. For each car worker with productivity incentives there was a sweatshop worker whose immiseration was guaranteed by less flexible employers and markets. For some this divided the class against itself: the specter of a Ford Anglia motor car outside a council house was enough to convince many a worker/socialist that consumerism bred class enemies the way education had done (and continued to even after the Butler Education Act of 1944).[5] Thus, the British worker was told that she or he had either disappeared, or become middle class—one of "Them." Not only is there no empirical data to support embourgeoisment as a general trend,[6] but theoretically, the affluence did not alter the position that the worker occupied in the productive process: the economic structure was still reproducing a proletarian role within capitalism that car or chemical workers, for instance, were still experiencing as "lived relations." Indeed, although this affluence itself was also being bought at the expense of Third World labor, it underlined the overall position of the English working class as one of continuing servitude.

Consumerism made the changes *seem* much more fundamental than they were. The consumption of goods did not occur evenly across the working class, but then such differences had already been regionally apparent for some time (particularly between standards of living of the North and South). It cannot be denied that historical perspective now allows us to see that the condition of the English working class improved, albeit unevenly through the fifties and sixties and that this has led to further stratification within the class; yet it would be hard for theorists of the right or left to claim that consumerism has proved emancipatory in any significant sense.[7] At a time when an increase in poverty and unemployment is matched by decreases in social services it is now much easier to realize that TV ownership has not released the working class from capitalist exploitation. Further analysis is required if we are to understand "the whirlwind of change" as Doris Lessing described the years under discussion.[8] In this light I want to consider some initial articulations of the "new problematic" that, to some extent, have conditioned all subsequent responses to this period, including mine.

In the previous chapter I looked at the implications of E. P. Thompson's *The Making of the English Working Class* as a paradigmatic model of agency that could be used to track the developments and mixed fortunes of working-class literary production. As indicated, Thompson's theory of agency is not unproblematic,[9] but this can be explained in terms of the historical conjuncture in which his project was attempted. If the theoretical productivity of Thompson's work was built on a socialist–humanist legacy, two other books of the period were mediated by similar circumstances—albeit with different implications and expressions.

Richard Hoggart's *The Uses of Literacy* appeared in 1957, a book about the changes in working-class culture written during a period when certain forms of working-class expression were gaining rapid cultural recognition. Hoggart maintains that working-class "affluence" had been achieved by a simultaneous cultural sterility, revealed in an analysis of the process of cultural "massification."[10] Of course, one immediately recalls the *Scrutiny* project, particularly the work of the Leavises and Denys Thompson: all raged against mass culture the way Matthew Arnold feared anarchy *without* culture. In this light, and without intention, Hoggart had pitched in with an ideological position that also sought to marginalize working-class culture, but where he made appeals for regional and folk forms, the Leavisites favored an elitist "tradition."[11] In addition because, as Hoggart maintained, socialism and labor organization remained largely abstract within the totality of working-class experience, party politics, the workplace, and unionization are not seen to be significant mediating factors of working-class culture. Yet for all this the book stands as a brilliant attempt to articulate the configurations and complexities of cultural *struggle*. That this struggle is undertheorized (for instance, in the more or less arbitrary or hypostatized categorization of class that runs through the section on "Them" and "Us") is primarily because Hoggart's sociological apparatus did not perceive working-class culture as a problem for theory. The most glaring lacuna in his book becomes, therefore, the absence of any discussion of the massification of culture in terms of broader structural transformations of the English working class to which I earlier referred, the terms indeed, in which "class" makes any historical sense.

Hoggart, however, is not alone in extracting class-specific culture as a sociological category from its network of social relations. If the British Left at the time was not disillusioned by the revelations of the Twentieth Congress and by the Russian invasion of Hungary, then nevertheless these moments did produce a form of disillusioned socialism where party politics generally were called into question (in the British Communist Party, this led to mass resignation), and class politics were hybridized into populist and community-interest forms (the CND movement was typical of this). And, for working-class intellectuals who no longer sensed the persuasive solidarity of a socialist movement, many, like Hoggart, turned to "culture" for evidence of struggle—not because it supported traditional notions of class warfare, but because cultural struggle somehow substituted for it. In Raymond Williams's early work we can see clear signs of this tendency to conflate culture as a site of struggle, with culture as the only struggle.

Williams's *Culture and Society* appeared in the same year as *Saturday*

*Night and Sunday Morning* but no study to date has seen them as mediated by similar historical relations. Both works are interventions by working-class writers, the first in the rarefied air of English academe, the second in the equally selective world of the English novel. Both writers are keenly concerned with cultural debate. Both writers articulate a class purview that is bound by (1) experiences of poverty during youth, (2) the ardor of military service, and (3) the relative expansion of opportunities after the war (although, to be sure, Williams made a mark in academia before the Butler Education Act, and Sillitoe turned to writing with little education behind him). Both, of course, are writers of the Left, although Williams would probably agree more than Sillitoe on the shared interests such politics entail. The most important determinate relation, however, is the fact that neither writer wrote these works with working-class traditions to build on.[12] Williams, for instance, attempted a radical cultural critique from a Leftist position where Christopher Caudwell might seem his most obvious predecessor, a writer who, as Williams remarks in *Culture and Society*, was "not even specific enough to be wrong."[13] For his part, Sillitoe writes working-class fiction "rooted in his own experience" with few works as literary inspiration in mind—"The whole proletarian movement in literature before the war or between the wars really failed—with the possible exception of Walter Greenwood's *Love on the Dole*, which was a good book."[14] The innovations of both writers are, to some degree, determined by a lack of received alternatives, which is another way of saying that the limitations of their differing work is produced by the same underdeveloped or marginalized traditions. Yet I want to consider how Williams's work in some sense prepares the ground for understanding Sillitoe's.

*Culture and Society* begins by discussing five key words—industry, democracy, class, art, and culture, but in fact, it is only really about the last two, and even then art is explained as a function of culture and its tradition. Where Hoggart initiated new perspectives on cultural change in the working class, Williams sought to provide a history of the concept of culture itself that would point to "a full restatement of principles, taking the theory of culture as a theory of relations between elements in a whole way of life."[15] Where Hoggart talks of the massification of culture, Williams talks of the necessity of examining the idea of an expanding culture. Again, my point is not to make such comments say the same thing, but to see the period of my study as a turning point of sorts where the focus on "culture" and "working class" become mutually determinant acts of historical change. It is only through this complex set of interrelations that the impact of Sillitoe's writing can be understood. Thus, the work of Williams, Hoggart, and Thompson during this period is not necessarily a solution to the problems posed by articulating working-class culture, but can also be seen as part of the problem. As Richard Johnson has perhaps over-laconically put it:

The moment of culture can be understood as an attempt to vindicate critical social thought (from Marxism to Left Leavism) in an exceptionally hostile climate and in circumstances where even "the people" seemed content. Every single national resource was important in such an effort. What could English culture offer to stem the the tide of "Progress"? Answer: The Tradition. Answer: William Morris. Answer: The English working class in a more heroic phase.[16]

By tradition, Johnson means the tradition of culture as outlined in *Culture and Society* with, of course, its attendant sideward glance to Leavis and the Scrutineers.[17] The reference to William Morris implicates both Thompson's full-length work on Morris, and Thompson's and Williams's converging interests in radical forms of populism. The last "answer" refers to Thompson's monumental book on the working class. Culturalism, as it became known, emerged as a contradictory Leftist strategy, a plausible way out of the ideological constraints of vulgar Marxism that yet seemed to render political action necessary at the same time that it tended to underline a more general political quietism. In Williams, suspicion over the excesses of Russian socialism precipitated a suspicion of Marxism in general and the terms of its analysis in particular. Williams's often-quoted statement, "There are in fact no masses; there are only ways of seeing people as masses"[18] became, as Eagleton has pointed out, more categorical in *The Long Revolution:* "We can group individuals into particular classes, nations or races, as a way of refusing them individual recognition."[19] One cannot help but recall the number of times that Sillitoe has insisted on an authorial focus on the individual over and above the claims of class differentiation.[20] Neither Williams nor Sillitoe can be adequately assessed using the individual versus class model. I will discuss this in relation to Sillitoe's writing later, but here it should be stressed that even in *Culture and Society* the accentuation on individuality is not employed as a substitute for class analysis.

What Williams writes in *Culture and Society* does not dismiss class, but defends the working class or masses against uses of such categorization that marginalize their lived experiences or desires. Two examples will help to clarify this point. One objection to the use of "mass" occurs in its connection to democracy:

It is . . . the declared intention of the working people to alter society, in many of its aspects, in ways which those to whom the franchise was formerly restricted deeply disapprove. It seems to me, when this is considered, that what is being questioned is not mass-democracy, but democracy. If a majority can be achieved in favour of these changes, the democratic criterion is satisfied. But if you disapprove of the changes you can, it seems, avoid open opposition to democracy as much by inventing a new category, mass-democracy, which is not such a good thing at all. The submerged opposite is class-democracy, where democracy will merely describe the processes by which a ruling class conducts its business of ruling.[21]

While critics like Eagleton, Johnson, and Barrett are correct in their misgivings about Williams's organicism, particularly concerning the febrile life of working-class communities, there is something disingenuous about their varied accusations regarding "class" in *Culture and Society*. If, on one level, *Culture and Society* purports to track the theoretical possibilities of four or five keywords like "democracy" described above in relation to class or mass, it does not follow that consideration of one term excludes class or mass. Rather, it is clear from the quote above that Williams is trying to undermine what he sees as a ruling class ideological use of such terminology in order to establish his own counter-position. This tactic is employed in a similar fashion late in Williams's argument:

> The question then, perhaps, is whether there is any meaning left in "bourgeois"? Is there any point, indeed, in continuing to think in class terms at all? Is not industrialism, by its own momentum, producing a culture that is best described as classless? . . . The basis of a distinction between bourgeois and working-class culture is only secondarily in the field of intellecural and imaginative work, and even here it is complicated, as we have seen by the common elements resting on common language. The primary distinction is to be sought in the whole way of life . . . between alternative ideas of the nature of social relationship.[22]

The theoretical inadequacies of this approach, the use of binary oppositions and so on, need not be discussed here. The point is that amongst the organic wholeness that marks Williams's prose (including his fiction), he nevertheless articulates the incommensurate differences between classes that legitimate a certain terminology and necessitate further analysis. The borders that Williams construes as dividing world views are not merely fictitious, although this does not discount the role of ideology in structuring difference (we see this in both Hoggart's and Sillitoe's descriptions of the "simplified sociology" of "us" and "them"); they are part of a concrete response to specific historical conditions: the changing constituency of the working class, a skepticism of orthodox Leftist beliefs, and a recognition that a culture for the masses is not synonymous with a culture by the masses. This does not constitute a theoretical position in any rigorous sense, but it does form a basis from which theory may be developed, a point that Eagleton, even in his most anti-Williams phase, is willing to concede.[23]

Certainly, Williams has subsequently made many contributions to that theoretical development—indeed, most of his career has been spent writing on the word *culture* in an increasingly theoretical comprehension of the term.[24] Having indicated at least some of the determinations of the "moment of culture" I would now like to make a contribution to the theoretical understanding of this moment. The historical bent of my approach will not necessarily agree with conventional cultural analysis of this period (as perhaps the preceding comments have already indicated). In this respect, I take my cue from Walter Benjamin:

"To articulate the past historically does not mean to recognize it 'the way it really was' (*Ranke*). It means to seize hold of a memory as it flashes up at a moment of danger."[25]

In *Culture* (1981) Williams sets out a systematic analysis of the components of cultural formations as part of a broader sociology of culture. A critique of the entire analysis need not detain us here. What interests me are Williams's criteria for classifying types of modern cultural formations.[26] He groups them according to two factors: their internal organization and their external relations. Each term is then subclassified. Thus, internal organization is based on (1) formal membership (e.g., guilds); (2) some collective public manifestation such as an exhibition, group press, or manifesto (e.g., the Pre-Raphaelite Brotherhood and its journal *The Germ*); and (3) a conscious association or group identification (e.g., Bloomsbury). External relations in cultural formations are then divided as follows: (a) specializing (promoting work in a particular form or style); (b) alternative (production facilities usually outside existing institutions); and (c) oppositional (where alternative modes are raised in *active opposition* to established institutions). As Williams admits, there are some crossovers here, in addition to which each classification is overdetermined by such factors as the means of cultural production (particularly as it pertains to "external relations"), the identification processes of "art" (one cultural formation's version of "art" may simply be "non-art" to others),[27] and the forms of expression available. Yet, although the cultural matrix suggested is certainly complex and juggles cultural heterogeneity in productive ways, a problem arises when these classifications for cultural formations and external relations are considered in terms of intentionality. It is useful to continually draw distinctions between intentionality and agency, especially when the working class feature in the analysis. That is, a group can be the agent of cultural production without their intentions being met. The categories that Williams suggests are all bound by notions of authorial intent, and the groupings therefore tend toward group existence as a product of that intent. This, however, does not explain that much-maligned cultural formation, the Angry Young Men, to which Sillitoe's name is often and so misleadingly applied. In this light, I will add a fourth category to Williams's formulations—a cultural formation based on determinants that produce a group identification even if the "members" themselves are opposed to the terms or the very idea of a "formation." Such a formation is mediated as what I will call a *cultural event*. It differs from the other categories because its organization is primarily external to the members grouped within it. Individual authorial intentions may well correspond on occasion with these external organizing principles and thus the "members" may seem to contribute to or support a cultural formation that is nevertheless never quite their own. If such a grouping can be said to be oppositional, then this can be because and in spite of active participation. In what follows I will argue that the Angry Young Men phenomenon is a cultural event that has profound implications for understanding the intervention posed by working-class writing in the late fifties and early sixties.

An initial point that underlines that the cultural event is part intention and much construction concerns the term "Angry Young Man." Leslie Allen Paul has claimed first use of the phrase, having published an autobiography in 1951 called *Angry Young Man*.[28] By some quirk of history the book is a story of a Marxist moving from class war through the twenties and thirties to eventual Christian conversion. It is not that the Angries were devout Christians, but the flight from political orthodoxy becomes a definable feature of those writers who were politically inclined. And then, on May 8, 1956, John Osborne's *Look Back in Anger* was staged at the Royal Court Theatre, London—and for some, at least, the rest is history.

Yet for all the brouhaha about Osborne's play and Mr. Paul's handy label, the roots of the Angry Young Men, as cultural event, lie in a cultural formation distinctly other than the cultural event: The Movement. The Movement, as Blake Morrison has shown in his book of the same name, displays much more coherent internal organization than its offshoot.[29] But the similarities and differences in stance are nevertheless instructive. Like the Angries, Movement members considered themselves enemies of the old order, but one can tell that their nonconformism was based on an emergent conformity: "Genuflections towards Dr Leavis and Professor Empson, admiration for people whom the thirties by-passed, Orwell above all (and, for another example, Mr Robert Graves) are indeed signs by which you may recognize the Movement."[30] The penchant for Leavis, Empson, and Orwell is conditioned by a sense of their anti-Establishment criticism (whether Establishments of the Left or Right) particularly with regard to poetry, the Movement's main form of cultural production. Like the Angries, the Movement was quickly attacked as a journalistic invention, "a gigantic confidence trick" and a "publicity campaign," in this case allowing "fame hungry" poets to promote "themselves by means of a group name."[31]

The governing characteristics of the Movement members are their lower-middle-class background, their Oxbridge education, and their birthdates (mostly in the early twenties). This class fraction in England, the petty bourgeoisie, also produced members for the Angries with the same qualifications (like Lindsay Anderson and Stuart Holroyd), and also (here the connection is most obvious) the same members (John Wain and Kingsley Amis being the most notable). Unlike their predecessors in the thirties they were decidedly not *engagé* and their liberalism went only so far as "neutralism" in politics. Their rise to prominence in the developing Cold War of the fifties is in many ways symptomatic of a general decline in Britain's role in world politics (many of the Movement were "little Englanders"), a rolling back of Britain's imperial past with all the upper-class attitudes that that encompassed, and most importantly the concomitant cultural concerns that had nourished and sustained such ideology. Donald

Davie, a self-proclaimed spokesperson for the Movement, sees the last point as crucial: "[The Movement's] sociological importance is very great, and it consists in this—that for the first time a challenge is thrown down, not by individuals like Lawrence, Arnold Bennett, Dylan Thomas, but by a more or less coherent group, to the monopoly of British culture sustained for generations by the London haut-bourgeois."[32] According to Williams's classifications, here we have a cultural formation of the third type whose "external relations" can broadly be defined as "oppositional." In addition, the Movement could claim unified forums for their work through *First Reading* (1952–53), a series of radio programs under the auspices of John Wain, *Poets of the 1950s* (1955), edited by D. J. Enright, and *New Lines* (1956).

The reason the Angry Young Men *seems* like a similar cultural formation to the Movement is in part because it is merely an extension of it. But the most stark difference between the two is the specific moments in which they make their appearance. In the cultural doldrums that followed the Second World War any movement that challenged the stultifying pretence of the Right-wing orthodoxy, resplendent up to and through the pages of *London Magazine* and *Encounter*, was bound to appear radical, as a liberal among reactionaries usually does. But alas, Amis's Jim Dixon is separable from Osborne's Jimmy Porter not because their politics are immensely different, but because, after Suez and the invasion of Hungary, the critical estimation of political questions changed. Suddenly, there were a host of "good brave causes" to chase down. But the bourgeois liberalism that had previously contributed to the Movement's unity now, among the Angries, became much more diffuse, for now one had issues with which to properly flex one's political choice: one now had something to get angry about. Without these political events it would not be out of the question to wager that *Look Back in Anger* would have become an act of post-Movement blues—a kind of Movement on the wild side with Colin Wilson's *The Outsider* as its angst-ridden shadow. But after 1956 the cultural niceties of political neutralism would seem as reactionary as the parlor-room politics that it sought to oppose. To be *engagé*, then, was now in: the problem was to identify a set of cultural producers who took a similar view of things. It was in the search for cultural expression that met the demands of a new situation that the Angry Young Man was born.

In 1957 Tom Maschler edited a group of essays by writers broadly associated with the term "Angry Young Men." The title of the collection is *Declaration*, which at once suggests a manifesto according to Williams's second type of cultural formation. Maschler's introduction, however, attempts an immediate disclaimer:

We have to thank an even lower level of journalism for the phrase "Angry Young Men" which has been employed to group, without so much as an attempt at understanding, all those sharing a certain indignation against the apathy, the complacency, the idealistic bankruptcy of their environment. Thus the writers who have set themselves the task of waking us up have been rendered harmless in the Angry Young Men cage. . . . It is important to note that although most of the contributors to this volume have at some time or other been termed Angry Young Men they do *not* belong to a united movement. Far from it: They attack one another directly or indirectly in these pages.[33]

Note the contrast between Maschler's view and Davie's: here is a "movement" marked by disunity, yet it can claim among its personnel some of the same writers as before. John Wain, for instance, whose work for *Essays in Criticism* (despite what he says) places him firmly in the Movement camp has an essay in *Declaration*. Here, Wain's ideological position is in step with his earlier work, a point evident even in the title of his contribution, "Along the Tightrope." As before, Wain recommends "keeping our heads," yet now Movement neutralism is held up as Angries activism. On such shaky contradictions a cultural event becomes established. Where Lindsay Anderson can write "This virtual rejection of three-quarters of the population [the working class] of this country represents more than a ridiculous impoverishment of the cinema. It is characteristic of a flight from contemporary reality by a whole, influential section of the community" (p. 141)—John Wain can write "the English working class have never been less fed in their history; all they are interested in is wringing higher and higher wages out of the bankrupt industries that employ them, with never a thought about altering the social structure in any way" (pp. 74–75).

What is so frightening about the *Declaration* collection is that the sharp disagreement among the pieces is somehow held up to be a virtue and that ultimately any method of being *engagé* will do, as long as it is your own way. Thus, in an essay called "A Sense of Crisis," Stuart Holroyd unswervingly proclaims that "freedom is an inner condition" and that "freedom is power over oneself" (p. 163). Holroyd's sense of crisis is personal and, although such politics have their own specific validity, his personal touch drains other political positions of any mutual assurance, of any solidarity. When Osborne writes, "I am not going to define my own socialism. Socialism is an experimental idea, not a dogma; an attitude to truth and liberty, the way people should live and treat each other. Individual definitions are unimportant" (p. 65)—one gets the impression that he perceives his cultural interventions as a much more collective expression, and that to be *engagé* means to be engaged with others in a struggle to change the world they see. Yet among all the hotch-potch of ideas and remonstrations that *Declaration* represents, any counter-position is undermined by further counter-counter-positions. In *King Lear* the Fool chides Lear that he is a nought without addition. Here the effect is similar: the pieces do not add up because each contribution is predicated on a unifying principle that stands as a veritable zero, the "Angry Young Man." Yet much can be made of nothing.

Robert Hewison's comment here is relevant: "Although Maschler is quick to denounce the lower level of journalism that produced the phrase 'Angry Young Man,' *Declaration* also exists to exploit this nonexistent person's success."[34] Indeed, to the extent that these writers perpetuate their association with a particular term by taking issue with it, *Declaration* is as clear a statement as any of a certain complicity. But we should also attempt to explain why the term always neutralizes the aims of the individual writers roped in by it, even when their association or pursuit is "active." It is impossible to argue that the Angry Young Men is a cultural formation with any group identity: this is the reason for exploring it as a cultural event, whose determinations by the media (interviews or attacks in the press and on TV) and by film (many of the key works of these authors were made into movies, which is one reason why I later analyze the film version of Sillitoe's *Saturday Night and Sunday Morning*) together suggest a much more complex sociocultural system. In this light, I want to consider how the Angry Young Men, as cultural event, "produces" Sillitoe.

Alan Sillitoe has always abhorred labels, accurate or otherwise, so it is not surprising that he takes issue with the term Angry Young Man. His comments, however, are particularly instructive given Maschler's early disclaimer: "[Angry Young Man] was just a journalistic catch-phrase. Nobody should have taken it seriously, but then people jump onto catch-phrases because it helps them to classify certain people and render them harmless."[35] The similarity here is striking. Sillitoe's criticism that labels render harmless "certain people" is precisely the reaction that allows him to be joined to the ranks of mislabelled Angries. John Wain, in a rare moment of interpretive verve, provides further explanation about the politics of naming: "In England there is a time-honoured method of dealing with opposition. First of all, you try to squash it: then, if it refuses to be squashed, you institutionalize it. Give it a name, turn it into an institution, and you find yourself absolved for ever from the responsibility to answer its criticisms."[36] In almost all the criticisms of the Angry Young Men label, including Hewison's excellent cultural analysis, it is unclear who is doing the labelling. Obviously the reviewers of the time have a lot to answer for, but we can hardly ascribe this cultural formation to their conscious intention. What emerges, however, is that after the initial exchanges over the importance of Osborne's *Look Back in Anger* the Angry Young Men phenomenon becomes a composite of contradictory viewpoints that together takes on an unconscious life of its own, as if, once set in motion, the cultural event is a self-perpetuating act that highlights certain cultural production, only to defuse its patent implications. The cultural event is an orchestration with no conductor, a symphony with no movements. In a period when the haut bourgeois had become increasingly hesitant about their position as arbiters of taste (in the university, in the art world, in music, in the theater) the cultural event appears as a structural substitution, an unconscious cultural intervention that, like a veritable Black Hole, sucks any conscious alternatives into it. What is interesting is that this generally reactionary process has progressive possibilities. If the Angry Young Men became a rallying point for various attacks on Establishment views it is clear that initially such attacks were the product of a petty-bourgeois nonconformity. But, of course, the period also sees the restructuring of the working class who, as consumers, now demand more than ever that their tastes be met and, as producers, are looking for ways to enter the more general sphere of cultural debate. What happens in the late fifties is that writers who previously might have found it extremely difficult to bypass the elitist pretensions of the culturati now found themselves swept into the center of the cultural arena. Unlike the moments I discussed in the previous chapter, here working-class writing was welcomed *en masse* as if it were the cutting edge of cultural expression.

The problems with this event, however, are manifest. First, the working-class fiction of these years was very different from that of the *Declaration* writers. Thus, as Ingrid von Rosenberg astutely points out, "this grouping led to a disregard of such books that told a different story from the recurring theme of the discontented scholarship boy."[37] In other words, if working-class writers have been shuffled in under the umbrella term Angry Young Men, literary history has not yet explained their presence; indeed, in most accounts the working-class contribution is explained away. I do not believe that the working-class writing of this period can merely be extricated from the cultural event in which it is so clearly enmeshed. It is far more useful to track its fortunes in relation to other components of the national culture. The event occurs in the hope that it will soon be over. Fortunately, such ideological staging can never quite secure the closure it desires. Thus, as Wain observed, some institutional adjustments are made, but these further highlight the radical potential that institutionalization hopes to dissolve.

Although the working-class writing does not constitute a movement, it nevertheless shares some governing characteristics. The first and most important of these is the language employed, and that is why it is the main focus of the next three chapters on Sillitoe. Here working-class subjectivity is conveyed in language appropriate to that world view, and not an approximation of it. This does not mean, however, that the social purview of these writers is somehow homogenous; it is rather that a heterogeneity of working-class concerns and ways of expressing them are given voice across a range of cultural producers. In addition, the themes of these works collectively contribute to a general view of the social situation of the working class that I attempted to map earlier. In the works themselves such themes are developed at what we may call the microsocial level.[38] The effects of the new affluence can be traced through many of these works in a double-edged fashion. On one level, books like John Braine's *Room at the Top* (1957) and David Storey's *This Sporting Life* (1958) feature leading characters whose ambition is only matched by their fear of failure. Other figures, like Arthur in *Saturday Night and Sunday Morning*, are as suspicious of the social climbers as they are rebellious about the old ways (and thus also may resort to an individualism often connected with the "I'm alright, Jack" ideology fostered by the Conservative party from the mid-fifties on). Much of the writing underlines that affluence in the working class was relative, and uneven. For instance, unwanted or accidental pregnancy as a theme highlights that the welfare state only went so far in providing health care, and that for many women characters—Brenda in *Saturday Night and Sunday Morning*, Jo in Shelagh Delaney's play, *A Taste of Honey*—this means continued hardship.

Another recurring theme is the strain on community caused by the new mobility. Both Arthur Machin in *This Sporting Life* and Lennie Hawk in *The Blinder* are ambivalent about the heroic position that sports stardom affords them. If both represent the working-class hedonism identified by Hoggart, they are yet torn by an underlying sense of community responsibility and worry about how they fit in. Of course, it is no coincidence that changing community interests feature in Raymond Williams's contribution to this writing, particularly the novel *Border Country* (1960) which in many ways is better testimony to the relationship between culture and community than his celebrated critique two years earlier. Crossing the border, for Williams, is usually a one-way process where commmunity interests are threatened by people like Matthew in the story moving on (and it is here that scholarship boy stories and worker affluence narratives converge). Matthew's identity crisis is based on a fear that his consciousness will not remain faithful to the community in which it was formed. In some ways this is an odd formulation, yet it typifies a certain essentialism in much of this literature's expression of community. Other books of this period also show, however, that working-class solidarity is not essentially dependent on prewar community relations. True, there is a sense of loss, but this does not eradicate the potential gain from change. The fragmentation becomes for many writers, here Jack Common and Sid Chaplin come to mind, a reason to write, not just from some nostalgic longing, but from a desire to articulate the changing face of working-class experience. Much of the power of this writing lies in its steadfast ability to record the minutiae of everyday working-class existence as a barometer both of continuity and change. I hope this becomes more evident in my later discussion of specific works by Sillitoe. Here I am interested in how the necessity to express the working class is enmeshed with a concomitant necessity to handle working-class expression.

Apart from common thematic elements in their work, these writers share a genuine dilemma in their role *as* writers. In his essay "The Author as Producer," Walter Benjamin raises some important issues about the role of the committed writer, and indeed provides some of the theoretical inspiration to my final chapter. Here it is interesting to note that his thesis on literary *tendency* depends on examples where the authors, or intellectual producers, are of bourgeois origin—which leads him to comment:

> Even the proletarianization of an intellectual hardly ever makes a proletarian. Why? Because the bourgeois class gave him, in the form of education, a means of production that, owing to educational privilege, makes him feel solidarity with it, and still more it with him. Aragon was thereby entirely correct when, in another connection, he declared, "The revolutionary intellectual appears first and foremost as the betrayer of his class origin."[39]

What of working-class intellectual producers? Do they, by entering the bourgeois cultural sphere of production, become bourgeois themselves or remain resolutely in solidarity with their class origins? To what extent does the business of fiction, of which the cultural event is its late capitalist formation, entail the betrayal of class origins? The answers to these questions do not form the mirror image to Benjamin's example. One reason is that working-class writers bring to their production a different set of tastes and distinctions. For the bourgeois intellectual who is pro-proletarian the task is to adapt her or his cultural capital toward social transformation; for the working-class equivalent the prospect is much more daunting because such producers begin from a point where they have little or no cultural capital with which to initiate this intervention. Their task, to borrow from Pierre Bourdieu, is to transform their *habitus into* cultural capital while at the same time calling into question the latter category.[40] I would suggest that the process of this transformation depends little on volition (indeed, declared intent often becomes a hindrance). In fact, the frustration that many of these writers experienced during arguably their most "successful" period underlines that willing participation only seemed to strengthen their containment by processes necessarily, but not absolutely, beyond their control. The paradox of the cultural event is that it seeks working-class cultural participation with or without volition. Yet it is not simply cultural manipulation because it can never fully control what it stages.

The cultural event lays bare the cultural contradictions of late capitalism, for each attempt to stage a new or alternative cultural component of life calls into question the norms of cultural orthodoxy. To capitalize on the Angries meant giving space to opposition from the margins, which at the same time exposes a recognition that marginal culture demands this space. In this light the cultural event is determined by social phenomena broadly analogous to Gramsci's notion of hegemony. Gramsci maintained that a dominant group can produce a "spontaneous consent" in the working classes consistent with that group's hegemonic function in the world of production. Stuart Hall here notes how the hegemonic relates to the cultural in Gramsci:

Hegemony implied that the dominance of certain formations was secured, not by ideological compulsion, but cultural leadership. It circumscribed all those processes by means of which a dominant class alliance or ruling bloc, which has effectively secured mastery over the primary economic process in society, extends and expands its mastery over society in such a way that it can transform and refashion its ways of life, its mores and conceptualization, its very form and level of culture and civilization in a direction which, while not directly paying immediate profits to the narrow interests of any particular class, favours the development and expansion of the dominant social and productive system of life as a whole.[41]

On one level, that of content analysis of the literary production in question, it is notable that the logic of consumer capitalism has become a rationale for daily conduct: the logic of affluence indeed, has been introjected. It is as if the working-class writing of this period is documentary evidence of the "contradictory consciousness" of consent that hegemony seeks to muster. On a more fundamental level, however, that of language, cultural leadership is almost bound to pull the rug from under its own feet for, as I will demonstrate clearly in the following chapters, the task of asserting a hegemonic use of language is always already undermined by language as a shared body of signs. Class interests intersect in sign as Volosinov shows, because a class can never monopolize sign. What hegemonic cultural relations can attempt to do, of course, is monitor the avenues through which cultural expression is disseminated. Cultural struggle is in this sense a struggle over access to the means of signification which themselves are the bearers of cultural capital. Thus what hegemony cannot achieve at the level of language it attempts to assert at the level of cultural formation, the means by which particular language uses can get a wider audience. One must, however, avoid reducing the cultural event, as a manifestation of cultural hegemony, to being a function of dominant culture. In the "whirlwind of change" that I have tried to trace, the cultural event does not emerge as a mere cog in a machine, its operations are much too diverse and fluid. It seeks consent in the most contradictory ways by attempting to embrace and subsume the very cultural expression that calls it into question. It is as if the lion tamer wants to wake the lion to produce a performance, but avoid the fact that the lion is stronger. One hardly needs reminding that hegemony continually renegotiates working-class consent, just as the working class itself helps to stubbornly redefine its agency.

Can we ascribe a source to particular hegemonic cultural relations, an origin for the cultural event? Because there is never unilateral agreement between and within institutions of cultural production and dissemination, one cannot point the finger and say the Arts Council is the culprit, or *TLS*, or the BBC, or Oxbridge. Indeed, it is not a question of affixing guilt, but one of understanding the complex network of relations that together constitute the staging of the cultural event. Market considerations play a key factor here. For many publishers during the fifties, it was simply business as usual: they continued to reject ninety-nine out of one hundred manuscripts. In *Books and Publishers* Michael Lane shows how this evaluative stage was not just conditioned by the profit motive, but also by individual editors wishing to promote "cultural standards."[42] Since it is almost impossible to track the fortunes of rejected manuscripts, we can only go by what did reach the bookshelves. Certainly, even if we bracket the working-class writing of the period, the art of fiction was very much alive (if not kicking). A list of novelists that includes C. P. Snow, Anthony Powell, Iris Murdoch, Doris Lessing (whose contribution to *Declaration* underlines the mystifying role of the label Angry Young Men), William Golding, Angus Wilson, and Muriel Spark can hardly be described as lackluster. In drama, of course, there was much more reason for complaint, which served to pitch *Look Back in Anger* further into the spotlight. In this respect, two factors are important: the relative torpor of English drama in contrast to particularly European experimentation, and the flexibility that allowed alternative forms and theater opportunities to develop (here the Arts Council was much more influential than in the novel).

As early as 1946 George Devine (artistic director of the English Stage Company) had appealed, "Here and now we are ready to do something new. . . . We'll play with anyone who is honest."[43] Ten years later, with the financial backing of a businessman, Neville Bond, Devine's company opened its doors at the Royal Court Theatre and in its first season decided to take a chance on a play by a little known writer, John Osborne. Another significant moment of 1956 was Joan Littlewood's Theatre Workshop production of Brendan Behan's *The Quare Fellow,* a play with more deep-down vehemence than any of the more recognized "Angry" writing. Both the English Stage Company and the Theatre Workshop played key roles in the promotion of working-class expression in the fifties. For instance, Arnold Wesker's *The Kitchen* and his trilogy were staged by Devine's company. Meanwhile, Theatre Workshop, with more openly Leftist politics and, therefore, shoestring budgets to match, continued to take chances on working-class plays, the most prominent being the staging of *A Taste of Honey,* a first play by nineteen-year-old Shelagh Delaney. Not only is Delaney's play a powerful indictment of the all-encompassing affluence thesis of the fifties, but it provides a strong feminist critique with a working-class outlook. Her play is an important reminder that the patriarchal ideology that fetishized the Angry Young Men was often perpetuated in the working-class writing of the period, and that includes the work of Sillitoe, Storey, and Barstow. It should not be forgotten that much of the fame of male working-class writers rested on the relative silencing of working-class women. In fact, it can be shown that the institutional flexibility of the British theater in the fifties provided easier avenues than the novel and its publishers for marginalized culture.

Why the novels gained such great cultural capital was not so much because publishers took a risk on working-class writing but because they achieved wide popular appeal through film versions with paperback tie-ins. I will discuss this at greater length in relation to *Saturday Night and Sunday Morning* in chapter 5, but here one should note that the market was quite clearly consumer-driven. What was inadvertently discovered was that the working class watched films and read paperbacks in much greater numbers than they went to the theater or bought or borrowed hardbacks. Although one cannot discount the role of a growing lower-middle-class audience (many with working-class roots) in the popularization of working-class writing, working-class consumers, and especially the young, made up a significant proportion of those who supported the projection of their lives on screen and in books. *Saturday Night and Sunday Morning, Room at the Top, A Taste of Honey, Look Back in Anger,* "The Loneliness of the Long Distance Runner," *A Kind of Loving, Billy Liar,* and *This Sporting Life* were all made into successful films and paperbacks.[44] The cultural event suggests that the logic of capitalism is in direct contradiction to the logic of cultural hegemony—unless this itself questions whether the works above constitute an effective counter-hegemonic cultural sphere.

The prospect that working-class writing can merely be staged as the event of some broadly hegemonic cultural apparatus would not seem to bode well for the effectivity of political culture—not just by literary producers on behalf of the working class, but by working-class writers themselves. To counter this I have stressed that the containment system that the cultural event appears to offer falls far short of clearly defined cultural repression. One of the major lessons of the cultural event is that, unlike the moment of Chartism and the proletarian fiction of the thirties, we can no longer depend on models of political crisis as the basis for working-class cultural intervention,[45] and that the cultural logic of late capitalism—which I will address in more detail in my final chapter—fragments cultural opposition by offering it up as a homogenous or unified event or movement. The cultural event is thus not the mark of political crisis but perhaps more significantly a process that seeks to avoid such confrontation.

I began this chapter with a discussion of two important works by Hoggart and Williams and, although we may seem to have traveled some distance from those books, they are crucial to our understanding of the period. With subsequent contributions Williams has underlined the importance of his cultural critique to a theory of working-class fiction. To that end, building on his notions of cultural formation does not seem an option but a necessity. The idea of cultural event is an initial response to the challenge that his work represents.

Ultimately theorizing the cultural event may do no more than to make strange accepted forms of historical account, to brush history against the grain as it were. Many questions remain. For instance, how does working-class fiction, itself a product and producer of contradiction, resist the accommodating pretensions of literature as spectacle? Such resistance is not critically discernible at the level of form, a subject to which I will return. Certainly one could argue that the content of this fiction sufficiently distances the acceptable bounds of the "literary." But, as I suggested earlier, the greatest challenge of working-class fiction rests in its language. In the next three chapters, therefore, I will move from the historical determinants of cultural formation to the concrete utterances of working-class language. That I focus on the work of Alan Sillitoe is not meant to diminish the contributions of other writers, but allows a relatively close textual analysis of a writing foregrounded by history. In Sillitoe's signs we do not read the complete social situation of a class, *reductio ad absurdum,* but in the "spontaneous philosophy" of his language and the "structure of feeling" that it enunciates there is a language use that cannot be understood as just class-bound yet cannot be adequately interpreted beyond class either. In these two chapters I have tracked some of the historical relations in which Sillitoe emerges. The point now is to provide textual analysis without losing sight of those relations.

# 3

# The Apostle of Industrial Unrest:
# Alan Sillitoe's "The Good Women"

This chapter will present a reading of Alan Sillitoe's work that builds on the period study just described. The first part addresses two issues in particular: (1) What role can Bakhtinian theory play in an analysis of working-class writing? (2) What features of Sillitoe's work does such theory help to elucidate? The next chapter focuses on *Saturday Night and Sunday Morning,* and provides a detailed textual analysis that deepens our understanding of the "dialogism of the oppressed" while initiating a discussion of the working-class novel as form. Both parts are broadly Bakhtinian, although other aspects of radical theory will also be heard, particularly with an eye to the essay on theory that ends this book.

For radical theorists, particularly Marxists, Bakhtin represents insoluble theoretical problems. On the one hand, his theory of sign is resolutely historical, providing opportunities for concrete discourse analysis that at the same time is open-ended in a way that allows it to be enlisted in the name of a leftist deconstruction, *sans* Derrida.[1] Yet the cornerstone of Bakhtinian theory, dialogism, is posited as a refusal of theoretical transcendence of the subject which simultaneously undermines metaphysical idealism as it renders monological that mainstay of materialist approaches to literary production, dialectics, a subject to which I will return in due course. For a Marxist to wax Bakhtinian therefore, is not only to monologize the spirit of Bakhtin's work (that is, to attempt a closure of the "internal unfinishedness" of his theories), but is in some sense to be non-Marxist, or in the haute couture world of contemporary theory—*post-Marxist.*[2] Of course, given Bakhtin's many-voicedness, it all depends on which of his books that you read, or more specifically which parts of his books that you read. This chapter does not allow for a detailed discussion of the politics of selection (a subject that I have broached elsewhere),[3] but I hope that in the brief notes that follow you hear a voice that insists on the political imperatives of such selection. Although not wishing to make Bakhtin a Marxist guru for a postmodern world (the nature of his work makes that untenable), the specific reading of Sillitoe that follows is also a strategic intervention on the Bakhtin debate that does not accept, as many a Slavic studies critic would have it, that any Marxism in Bakhtin's work is merely a convenient disguise.

Working-class writing has lacked sufficient theoretical attention. As I have indicated earlier, it is not that we could not put together some sort of bibliography on the subject, but rather that most radical left theory on literature is preoccupied with the great texts of the Western bourgeois tradition.[4] There are obvious reasons for this, not least of which is the attempt to destabilize and undermine the theoretical bases of that tradition within the institutional framework in which it appears seamlessly justified—academia. The negative effect of this emphasis, however, has been to enact a certain unconscious complicity in the marginalization of alternative cultural production. *Les cultures subalternes*[5] are not so much a silent presence in literary discourse, but a significant absence. Feminist and black literatures are beginning to receive the recognition, with all the political significance, that they deserve. Much working-class culture, however, is safely filed under "popular culture," and thus for some remains the least popular work under discussion. It is my contention that part, at least, of the problem of marginalization of working-class culture in the bourgeois academy is not just a result of the political constituency of that institution, but is also attributable to the poverty of theory on the value of such cultural production. This is where the theory of Mikhail Bakhtin becomes useful in "reading" Sillitoe.

Working-class fiction, a curious hybrid of literature, at least given the class origins of the novel and short story, is too often discussed as a type, or genre with a more or less agreed-upon content. This, I believe, is theoretically and politically a mistake. Such analysis renders working-class writing a compendium of generic content components which, although useful in any broader thematic argument, often fails to articulate the central distinction of working-class fiction, its language. The class characteristics of language *use* are one of Bakhtin's major concerns. Bakhtin recognizes in his critique of Saussure that language is a sign system, where a sign consists of a formal element and a meaning which the element conveys. But for Bakhtin, the sign is not arbitrary: it is constituent in a process of social development:

> Every sign . . . is a construct between socially organized persons in the process of their interaction. Therefore, the forms of signs are conditioned above all by the social organization of the participants involved and also by the immediate conditions of their interaction. When these forms change, so does sign.[6]

Although Bakhtin does not emphasize a one-to-one relationship between social organization and sign, it is clear that, unlike say, Gareth Stedman-Jones's conception,[7] the sign is referential in a suprareflectionist way.

Existence reflected in sign is not merely reflected but *refracted*. How is this refraction of existence in the ideological sign determined? By an intersecting of differently oriented social interests within one and the same sign community, i.e. *by the class struggle*. . . . Class does not coincide with the sign community, i.e. with the community which is the totality of users of the same set of signs for ideological communication. Thus various classes will use one and the same language. As a result, differently oriented accents intersect in every ideological sign. Sign becomes an arena of class struggle. . . . Each living ideological sign has two faces, like Janus. Any current curse word can become a word of praise, any current truth must inevitably sound to many other people as the greatest lie. This *inner dialectic quality* of the sign comes out fully in the open only in times of social crises or revolutionary change.[8]

I have quoted Bakhtin at length because his theory has some important implications for reading working-class signs: (1) a working-class writer's world view at a particular historical juncture is unlikely to be always synonymous with the social purview of her or his class; (2) such a writer's language does reflect the sign use of her or his class, but also (3) language often refracts the accents of the sign community necessarily outside her or his class. In the gaps and intersections between these three sets of relations the class struggle is being enacted at the level of language, although it is clear from my previous analysis that I do not agree that these struggles are necessarily most pronounced during periods of crisis. Since every sign is to be fought over, the language of class is constituted not by a definable body of words (however ideology may present this as such), but by a series of what we can provisionally call "class effects": ruptures, discontinuities, and slippages in meaning between the use of language by one class and its use by another that give both their distinctive character. Language is the major cultural capital of class.

How can Bakhtin's concept of dialogism enhance a theory of working-class fiction based on the above critique of sign? With a veil perhaps. The language of working-class fiction is always already dialogized to the extent that it is a cultural product self-conscious of its marginal status. Working-class fiction expresses social meaning in a way that not only communicates a sense of class-specific idioms, but deterritorializes language beyond those idioms. Thus, although dialogism cannot be reduced to class per se, as "an arena of class struggle" dialogic signs nevertheless have class effects. What should be addressed in such fiction is not an illumination of social dialect sui generis, but, to borrow from Bakhtin, the "dialogic angles" in which various styles and dialects are counterposed and put to use: "dialogic relationships are only possible between language styles, social dialects, and so forth, insofar as they are perceived as semantic positions, as language worldviews of a sort."[9] This dialogic semantic doubling within the individual utterance is of immense importance to the analysis of working-class writing in particular, and cultural production in general, for I believe it can be shown how working-class language dialogizes according to historically specific social situations; that is, how its semantic positioning doubles in response to and as interventions against perceived cultural institutions of production and reception. This is the "dialogism of the oppressed."

Dialogism, however, is not a synonym for dialectics as Bakhtin and Bakhtinians since have been at pains to point out: "Dialogue and dialectics. Season the words of a dialogue (the division of voices), season then the intonations (of a personal and affective character): shell abstract notions and reasonings from live words and sayings; wrap the whole in a unique abstract consciousness—and you get dialectics." As Tzvetan Todorov suggests, Bakhtin's view here reiterates a lifelong suspicion of the Hegelian dialectic as a unifying principle for everything, thus it is mocked as a monological potpourri.[10] Since we have already noted Bakhtin's insistence on the inner dialectic quality of the sign we should perhaps add that dialogue and dialectic are not mutually exclusive terms, but their coexistence in Bakhtin's theory is extremely problematic. For now I can do no more than suggest that the two terms mutually deconstruct each other: the dialectics of sign give the apparent ubiquity of dialogism a firmer historical basis, while the alterity of dialogism opens the all-consuming teleology of the dialectic to scrutiny. Perhaps, after all, this war of concepts is itself dialogic in nature, where we hear both a voice essential to the understanding of language, and another implicit to the meaning of revolution.

The reason Bakhtin made special claims for dialogism in the novel is that the novel provides the formal open-endedness necessary to appropriate and organize heteroglossia; that is, the sociohistorical elements that make a word utterance different from one place and time to another. Unfortunately, although the novel is indeed a special case, it is too much to hope that the novel is just a microcosm of heteroglossia (a problem that will be discussed in the following chapter in relation to *Saturday Night and Sunday Morning*). If feminist, and indeed Althusserian theory is useful in this regard, it is because both have shown that the silences of texts like novels and short stories are indicative of both what they want to say, but for ideological reasons are constrained not to say. Most criticism of this sort has attempted to give voice to what is unsaid in the text through a symptomatic reading that looks to another text necessarily absent from the first. To adequately explain the class purview of working-class fiction Bakhtin's theory of voicing must be tempered by a theory of silence;[11] for to understand the dialogism of the oppressed one must articulate the dialogism of the suppressed, those ideological and institutional relations that have often left working-class and women's utterances unuttered.

Before providing a reading in the light of the notions outlined above, I should add that there is a further interpretive adaptation of Bakhtinian dialogism that will be used. I refer here principally to the historically specific nature of the sign, which implies that the context of the verbal "utterance" is part of its material reality; it is only in this sense that it can be considered *living social intercourse.*[12] It is for this reason that, in what follows, I will be paying particular attention to the form in which this Sillitoe story was first published, because I believe it provides some clues to its significance as social discourse, both in its enunciation of certain "class effects" and in its self-conscious (and sometimes unconscious) dialogic perception of audience. My point is that the "speaking" working-class subject can only be understood as the product of a dialogic process of intersubjectivity; that is, in the dialogue *between* subjects.

"The Good Women" first appeared in a serialized form in the *Daily Worker* in 1962. The following year it was published in Alan Sillitoe's second collection of short stories, *The Ragman's Daughter.* In what follows I will mainly concern myself with the serialized representation of this story which I find particularly provocative given the theory outlined above.[13] "The Good Women" is about one woman in particular, Liza Atkin, a working-class woman from Nottingham: it is her story about coming to radical consciousness, but it is told from the perspective of an unidentified male within the narrative who is a friend of her son, Alf. This framing may appear harmless enough, but it raises some very important issues about the constitution of the woman as subject, and the working class as subject in language forms that may seem to serve neither. At a time when the subjectivity of both too often becomes a chimera that confirms nonexistence, and therefore, of course, nonexistence of the problem, I will attempt to show that the double marginality of Liza Atkin has a material existence in the language of this story, and that sign itself forms the arena in which her struggle is emergent.[14]

The story begins in the *Daily Worker* on Saturday, May 26, 1962. In the top right-hand corner of the page is a small picture of Alan Sillitoe and a brief biography. Sillitoe stares intently at a sheet of paper as if the words will form by looks alone. This is the image of the writer. In the center of the page is a large sketch of the top half of a woman. Her hair is unkempt, her arms are folded, her brow is furrowed, her eyes are worn, and her lips are tight. Like Sillitoe, she stares with determination; unlike Sillitoe however, it is unclear what she is staring at. She does not look directly at the reader; instead, her gaze is aimed somewhere other than at the reader. One may recall John Berger when he notes that, "seeing comes before words."[15] This woman is Liza Atkin. This drawing appears on page three which will later, in other worker dailies (*The Sun, The Daily Mirror*), become the site of a quite different representation of woman.[16] In Lacanian terms the semiotic difference between these representations appears to be that of the imaginary to the symbolic; but just in case this sounds too convenient we will add that both are cultural as well as psychological constructs, and although, for us, the symbolic appears to subsume all else before it, its propensity to represent the imaginary relationship of individuals to their real conditions of existence is, to say the least, highly problematic.[17] If we can say that Liza's subjectivity is overdetermined, it is as a symbolic representation which is itself always already a sociocultural product and site of production.

An excerpt of the story is quoted in large italics at the top of page three and serves to focus attention on the narrative: "These figures come to me out of the past, show themselves on the cell wall of my mind. They dominate the present also: vivid, large, common. Many of them are women, the good women, and though this story only concerns Liza Atkin, they attain the height of visions."[18] These visions are imagined by the first-person narrator as he lies in a prison cell. He has been arrested for "obstruction" while taking part in a "Ban the Bomb" demonstration in central London.[19] In the cell he remembers the Nottingham folk like himself: "They have lives to lead, and nothing will disturb their sublime preoccupation with it more than death or injury" (May 24, p. 23). The narrator remembers these folk as a community, and then, tellingly, introduces the subject of the good women. The association is that the good women are integral to the community spirit of the working class. A lot of weight therefore falls on the word "good," and the vision of Liza becomes its dialogic explanation.

Of course, it would be relatively easy to prove that the narrator's view of women rests in no small degree on stereotypic objectification, a masculinist idealization that both elevates and entraps women at one and the same time. Thus our first sight of Liza is one of the mother, complete with pram and two children. But, although this is seen as an unchallenged facet of Liza's everyday life, the narrative swerves away from pigeonholing Liza for being as good as a good mother should be. That she is a good mother therefore does not represent the totality of this "good woman" as the story develops; that is, a monologic proposition is overdetermined by a dialogic implication.

When we first hear Liza within the story she is making an appeal for community acceptance, an appeal marked by a language that is common to that sign community: "Hey, duck, what's it like living in this neighbourhood?" (May 24, p. 3). Liza's family has moved from another part of Nottingham in search of work. It is the Depression, and there can be no doubt that one reason, at least, for the flashback is to compare the condition of the British working class before and after the war. The family's poverty does not dim their pride: thus, Ted, the husband, "did not seem terrified of the workless world" and Liza fosters an interminable optimism, even when she has to explain away Ted's jobless condition by reference to a "serious illness." One should question, however, why his pride often leaves him sitting at home, while Liza's takes her to the rubbish tips with her trusty pram searching for wood, old rags, or metal. Such double standards underline the risk in the acceptance of a "good woman" proposed from a male point of view, even when Liza's actions themselves contribute to female bonding within the story: "She got on well with the women in the street, and would often hand out kindling wood brought back from the tips. 'Tek this till your husband gets a job, duck'" (May 24, p. 3).

Liza's struggle is continually marked by her relationship to working-class men and to officialdom. Too often, however, the former is deemphasized to highlight the latter. The reason for this revolves around the theme of solidarity: the male working-class narrator idealizes the working-class woman for standing tall in times of crisis. The narrator's "internal polemic," a critical component of double-voiced discourse,[20] accentuates a communal interest with Liza in the form of an unspoken ideological position, that of "us and them." Borrowing from Bakhtin, I am using "internal polemic" to mean that sideward glance of the narrative towards a hostile other—in this case, "them." It is internal because it is rarely outlined by the narrator's voice within the text, but this does not mean that the polemic does not have an effective ideological presence in the story. In *The Uses of Literacy,* Richard Hoggart describes how the ideology of "us and them" promotes definable community interests:

"Them" is a composite dramatic figure, the chief character in modern urban forms of the rural peasant-big-house relationships. The world of "Them" is the world of the bosses, whether those bosses are private individuals or, as is increasingly the case today, public officials. . . . "They" are "the people at the top," "the higher-ups," the people who give you your dole, call you up, tell you to go to war, fine you, made you split the family in the 'thirties to avoid a reduction in the Means Test allowance, "get yer in the end," "aren't really to be trusted," "talk posh," "are all twisters really," "never tell yer owt" (e.g., about a relative in hospital), "clap yer in clink," "will do y'down if they can," "summons yer," "are all in a click (clique) together," "treat y'like muck."[21]

That such positioning is an important way of understanding the "dialogism of the oppressed" can be further evidenced by Sillitoe's occasional prose on the subject. Indeed, the similarities in explication between Hoggart and Sillitoe on this point emanate from a similar class consciousness (although it is aimed at different audiences).[22]

The poor know of only two classes in society. Their sociology is much simplified. There are *them* and *us.* Them are those who tell you what to do, who drive a car, use a different accent, are buying a house in another district, deal in cheques and not money, pay your wages, collect rent and telly dues, stop for you now and again at pedestrian crossings, can't look you in the eye, read the news on wireless or television, hand you the dole or national assistance money; the shopkeeper, copper, schoolteacher, doctor, health visitor, the man wearing the white dog-collar. Them are those who robbed you of your innocence, live on your backs, buy the house from over your head, eat you up, or tread you down. Above all, the poor who are not crushed in spirit hate the climbers, the crawlers, the happy savers, the parsimonious and respectable—like poison.[23]

Of course, these divisions are historically specific: the lines of difference are continually being redrawn. It is interesting, however, that in "The Good Women" this sociology only exists as an internal polemic in the voice of the narrator; the external polemic is conveyed in the reported speech of Liza. While lauding Liza's position as spokesperson for her class we should stress that on this occasion it is made at the expense of, rather than alongside, a critique of patriarchal social relations. Thus, Ted is not seen as a source of Liza's oppressed position, whereas the Means Test Man is quickly identified as an enemy: "She knew he was trailing her, and every hundred yards or so through the streets she would turn and wave her fist: 'You stand bleddy need! You stand need, you lousy swine'" (May 28, p. 2). Significantly, however, it is Liza's brush with officialdom that inspires Ted to action, political action. Ted becomes an organizer for a worker's party and at election time comes around the neighborhood with a loudspeaker van handing out leaflets and newspapers: "He smiled at everybody, but his eyes were like fires burning on ice" (May 28, p. 2).

There is another explanation for the precarious role of Liza's voice in this story. The narrator's language continually enunciates the working class as subject. He does this both by description of the material conditions of that class according to different sociohistorical moments in its existence, and by the materiality of the language employed; the latter underlining that signs are common to more than one community of interest, but that social interaction gives to sign a specific accentuation which may define one interest in opposition to another. This, I believe, holds true as much for the working class as it does for women, but that is not the same as saying their interests are synonymous. What this can mean, however, is that at a certain historical conjuncture these interests may *appear* synonymous. This ideological wish-fulfillment helps to explain the narrator's predilection for Liza as the "good woman" and why, in this story, the narrator speaks for a class in general, and a woman in particular.

During the war, Liza takes care of a Welsh deserter, Robert, and hides him from the Redcaps as long as possible. It is an episode that supports both the antiwar flavor of the story and Liza's insistent solidarity with "us" against "them." It also conveys the political perspicacity of the proletariat. For a while Robert works as a window cleaner, but he also spends plenty of time in the local library seeking to find expression for why he had had enough of the war. His sketch appears in the second installment of Sillitoe's story. He wears an open, collarless shirt and a jacket. His face is animated and he appears to be addressing somebody, but not the reader. He points with the index finger of his left hand in order to underline his opinion. In his right hand he holds a book and, although the back cover of the book faces us, the title is inscribed upon it, *Crisis in World Politics*. Germany, Robert tells the narrator in the story, is going to lose the war because of economic collapse. Robert does not live to see the value in his prediction: he is killed while serving in the Merchant Navy. Although Robert's version of "us and them" is particularly idiosyncratic, its polemic is not lost on Liza, or even some, at least, of the readers of this form of the story.

Liza, meanwhile, continues to assert herself within and without the borders of what we take to be the narrative. To the right of this installment there is a review of a book, *Married Women Working,* where we read: "working wives have to maintain, as the survey puts it, 'determination, efficiency and sheer hard work' to cope with the demands of a job and a household." It continues: "And then, though the obvious reason for a wife working is because she needs the money, there are other factors involved. To counteract loneliness and the boredom of domestic chores, for example. As one 14-year-old is quoted as putting it: 'My own mother recently took up a part-time job, and I find that although she often feels tired and needs more help, she is much happier and has more interesting things to say'" (May 28, p. 2). As Sheila Rowbotham has pointed out in *Women's Consciousness, Man's World,* cultural values produce a lack of self worth in housework that is not as prevalent in work outside the home.[24] Liza recognizes this, both in words and actions.

After the war, both of Liza's sons were called up to do military service. After serving his tour, Harry, for want of anything better to do, decided to stay in the army another two years. He is killed in Korea by napalm during a mistaken air raid by American warplanes in search of communists. This incident is worth mentioning for three reasons. First, it provides further evidence that this story can be read as a critique of war, and the specific effects on the working class which is interpellated as its most integral subject. For example, earlier the narrator recalls the people of Nottingham who "don't want to kick the bucket for Berlin and the Germans, or for the English or the Americans or anybody, and who also don't want this threat of war hanging over them." Again, Liza "externalizes" such polemic: "Korea was a world, a word, as far off now as somebody else's dream, that had killed Harry, called him up and bombed him to ashes for no good reason, like when you have too many kittens you dunk some in a copper. It wasn't necessary, it was wrong, the bad thing to do" (May 30, p. 2).

The second point regards Sillitoe's description of Liza's reaction to this incident which, deliberately or not, is reminiscent of another writer of the working class, D. H. Lawrence. Thus, Liza's grief is measured like Gertrude's in *Sons and Lovers,* through Nature:

The lane narrowed, took her [Liza] through a field, over a stile and up a low hill, woods to the right and distant council houses to the far left. Clouds were low and grey like battleships, and the warmth hustled them along, making the grass move as well and smell fresh and hot like new bread. There seemed no end to things she could remember about him. A flicker of lightning festered over the black sky of Nottingham. Storms made her afraid, and she walked more quickly towards bus noises on the main road. I don't know who to blame, she thought, but go on, rip and claw the effing world to pieces. Tear up that bleddy town, sling it to hell. (May 30, p. 2)

For Liza, like Gertrude, the brush with Nature is both inspirational and cathartic, and leads to some form of resolve.[25] Of course, Woman/Nature communions are not politically unproblematic and one would not wish to make a virtue out of a seemingly reactionary intertextual relation; the point is that Liza does not sit well in the traditional molds that may be ascribed to her. In this light, the third point is related to the first two. So far, it may seem that I see the narrator of the story as having a monologic function in the narrative; that is, that he conceptually organizes all the voices that this text is meant to speak. Yet, I am trying to suggest that the voices of this text assume a polyphony, and that Liza, in particular, speaks beyond the intentions of narrative authority.

Soon after Harry's death Liza goes to work in a factory and, although no explanation is given within the tale, we can only assume that her loss has much to do with it. Her job is to check steel elbows with a gauge to measure for inaccuracy. It is interesting to note that the job is termed "viewing" and it is done predominantly by women. Although one can overemphasize this situating of woman as spectator to the products of capitalism, it is nevertheless significant that in this instance a sexist division of labor gives women a nonproductive role.

Liza soon becomes well known at the factory as the "apostle of industrial unrest." She also has particular importance for her fellow women workers: "Liza was a wag, life's fag lighter, wick, flint and fuel working in unison, a combustious spark tindering the whole line of women into laughs all day long" (May 31, p. 2). At one point, Liza climbs up onto the work bench and does a can-can. If her voice often seems to be drowned out by those of men, here it is muted by machinery. Thus, she dances to "the grinding roar of machinery, her singing mouth an apparition of silence among the total noise" (May 31, p. 2).

This apparition, this vision of a "good woman" finally comes to speak louder than language, in the sense that action may speak louder than words. The hours at the factory are shortened and shortened until the workers meet to discuss strike action. One speaker in particular moves Liza to tears: "He reminded her of Harry sprung back to life, and saying all the things he should have wanted to say because of his useless death, only now his face was harder because he'd been through the fire of it, and his words were sharp and loud because all uncertainty had been carried away by the possibility of some kind of action" (June 1, p. 2). Coming to consciousness, to a realization of the social relations in which the subject is inscribed, has been clumsily translated from Bakhtin as the "we-experience."[26] This collective consciousness is the product of the shared experience of an "objectively and materially aligned" group; in this case, the factory workers. It is for this reason that "The words and phrases, dull and empty perhaps to those who haven't worked in a factory, or owned one, thrilled Liza with their lucidity and common sense" (June 1, p. 2). Both Bakhtin and Sillitoe have been held to be too sociological in the elaboration of such shared experience: the former, on language; the latter, through language.

One only has to consider the political implications of not considering language in these terms to realize what is at stake here. Overlook the sociological dimension of Bakhtin's work and you have a dry and uninspiring functionalism: overlook this aspect in Sillitoe and he has no story to tell.[27]

When the workers leave the factory early, housewives ask Liza, "What's going off?" She replies, "We're on strike." "What for?" they ask. Liza answers, "We've had enough, that's why." Here again, Liza is the spokesperson for the workers, but it soon becomes apparent that her voice is more significant than that. When it comes to the mass demonstration, the other women from the line fail to appear; Liza concludes that they were either driven in by the rain or that they had shopping to do. At this point the narrator, having been out of Nottingham for five years, happens to be in town and decides to drop in on the demonstration. And, of course, the column of people attains the height of visions: "Many faces kept moving into recognition from the past. People who lived in our street, and neighbourhood, those I'd been to school with, the fathers of those I'd been with, and their brothers, with Liza walking for all the good women I'd known" (June 2, p. 3). Given that all the men in this procession are who they should be and Liza is more than herself, we can be forgiven for thinking that we are in the realm of the symbolic where, once more, Liza becomes the eternal maternal signifier. Perhaps it is more accurate, however, to see Liza here as a personification of a socially symbolic act since the narrator is also insistent that Liza is a worker involved in a strike and that her fellow workers and he draw inspiration from that.

The strike depicted in "The Good Women" has been the most controversial topic in critical discussion of this story (and the accidental bombing in Korea follows a close second).[28] Of course, a conflict between the workers and management would hardly be surprising to readers of the *Daily Worker,* although for arbiters of critical taste it has not been seen as relevant. Karl Miller has complained about Sillitoe's "forbidding intrusions," and Mordecai Richler wonders whether Sillitoe is "too gifted a writer to lapse into propaganda."[29] Bernard Lockwood is unequivocal: "The propaganda is arrived at circuitously by having a minor character address a group of strikers in a scene not at all important to the story, except that there is nothing else to the story except this propaganda. . . . Here, the reader is all too aware that it is Sillitoe himself, not any of his angry characters, standing on the soap-box lecturing to us."[30] This is a clear accusation of monologism, but it takes no account of the context in which the speech is delivered. As Bakhtin notes, "The immediate social situation and the broader social milieu wholly determine—and determine from within, so to speak—the structure of an utterance."[31] The strike speech is clearly explicable within its context, its language is dialogically angled with a particular audience in mind: it is the product of evaluative orientation rather than the semantic authority that "propaganda" implies. The "working-class effect" in this instance is dependent not only on an acknowledged community of interest within the story but also, of course, on social interaction with a reader. If we take the *Daily Worker* as a specific context for this type of utterance, there seems little reason to doubt that what Liza hears at the strike meeting will be read as what Bakhtin calls "active double-voiced discourse": in short, it will be read as one voice amongst other voices with a similar, though not synonymous, social purview. In another reading context, say, a volume of short stories, the internal polemic of the first instance may well be read as "forced" attack: a different "refraction of existence in the ideological sign" has been determined because different social interests are at work.

There is more to the narrator's vision of Liza and that is that Liza, in her struggle to exist, in her struggle to articulate that existence, comes to embody a revolutionary potential that the mutability of the sign in social interaction should serve to underline—though change is inevitable its nature is not. Thus, although the strike was won, Liza saw the struggle continuing: "You ain't won because you was too frightened to stay out and finish it." And later she rearticulates this spirit: "Maybe we'll end up having the same colour eyes. You never know, do you? There'd be no difference then between anybody. It's funny when you think of it like that. I wouldn't mind though, would yo' duck?" (June 2, p. 3). Of course, there are many examples in literary history that express a similar "will to equality," but it is rare that it is done with the conviction and articulation of the working class.

Bakhtin once wrote that "Consciousness takes shape and being in the material of signs created by an organized group in the process of its social intercourse. If we deprive consciousness of its semiotic, of its ideological content, it would have absolutely nothing left."[32] Part of what I've been suggesting here is based on this observation, that to understand Liza is to realize her consciousness as the product of social intercourse and not the other way around. Furthermore, working-class subjectivity, like women's subjectivity, is only comprehensible as a process of intersubjectivity in language. Therefore, although there is no definable body of working-class words, working-class enunciation can show the workings of class-specific social interaction at any one historical juncture.

Finally, I would like to underline that the dialogism of the oppressed can only be mapped in concrete historical terms, and that the utterance can only be understood as a node of social interaction which changes according to the context of that interaction. We have already noticed, for instance, how the *Daily Worker* (as utterance context), to some extent determines what I have called the working-class effects of "The Good Women." Like the context, the author too can produce these effects, but not as a mere reflection of individualized intent. It is with this in mind that I wish to consider the ending of "The Good Women" in the *Daily Worker,* an ending that is significantly different from the one that appears in hardback the following year.

It is not a question of which ending came first in Sillitoe's conception, although it is always interesting to note the sequence of such developments (the minor differences throughout the two versions suggest that the *Daily Worker* manuscript is indeed the earlier).[33] The major concern here is the dialogic angle of utterance altering in relation to context. As we have seen, this angle will alter irrespective of any change in the prose selected. On this occasion, however, the dialogic difference is compounded by Sillitoe's editing choices which, whether they directly reflect authorial intention or not, reaffirm collective interests with a given interlocutor.

> There are many good women in our area, and Liza was only one of them who lived a life worth thinking about on a long night like this. But if anybody ever asks me why I got hauled in by the coppers, why I don't believe in hydrogen bombs and the frightful waste and risk of nuclear bombs, and why I'd rather be Red any day than dead, then maybe I'll tell them about Liza Atkin. Certainly if anyone ever asked that last question of her, I know what she'd prefer. (June 2, p. 3)

This last paragraph of the *Daily Worker* version of the story is successful within the context of the rest of the tale. First, it underlines that Liza is one good woman amongst many, but that she has been the particular focus of the story. Second, the narrator reiterates the antiwar and "us and them" themes developed earlier. Third, the narrator expresses solidarity with Liza based on a recognition of shared interests. Although Liza has never espoused socialist principles, her words and actions bear an expressive relation to such tenets. This is not the product of some *deus ex machina* but is a mark of collective subjectivity in spite of the fact that both the narrator and Liza are presented as individualized subjects. It is important to note that the solidarity expressed is not seen as inevitable, but is contingent upon a mutual recognition, a recognition that is dialogized in the language of this story. Furthermore, the dialogic interaction of "The Good Women" must also be seen in the context of its presentation which, in the case of the *Daily Worker,* can only provide further potential for just this kind of recognition. If we can say that fiction is a mirror, it is but a shattered one: reader recognition is conditioned by which fragments she or he "sees," which in turn is overdetermined by the historically specific context in which that interaction takes place.

The version of the story that appears in *The Ragman's Daughter* omits most of the above paragraph and adds another scene. The narrator returns to the Nottingham area and meets Alf (Liza's remaining son) and his kids at a pub near Wollaton village. They talk and then, "The subject suddenly changed." Alf proceeds to talk about his mother and how she had helped the kids then continues:

"Mam was rough. In fact they didn't make 'em any rougher than mam. You remember that strike at the factory? I don't think she knew whose side she was on. I think she enjoyed it as well. The only complaint she'd got was that it worn't rough enough for her. She wanted a real blow-up. Mam was a good woman, I'll say that." He looked at his two kids fighting by the garage door: "Stop that, you little bleeders, or you'll get a pasting. Come on"—he turned to me—"you don't knock 'em back like you used to. I'll get a couple more."

"Thanks," I said, sliding the mug over. "Let's drink to Liza. She was one of the best."

"You can say that again"—keeping a good eye still on his kids. Then he hooked up the mugs and made for the pub's back door.[34]

This is not only the end of the story, but forms the last page of the book. Here the dialogic angle of address is altered, I would argue, according to different needs. That someone should echo the narrator's view of Liza as a "good woman" would seem at first superfluous, were it not for the fact that this is the voice of her son looking at her grandchildren. Do they represent the possibility of the "real blow-up" that Liza desired? If this is so there is little to support it in the rest of the story. In addition, although Alf too appreciates Liza's radical perspective it is not with the socialist solidarity intimated by the narrator. My point is not to decide which ending is better because this would be to lose the sense of the specific contexts in which they are inscribed. If the voice of the second version is less revolutionary in spirit, however, it is because it attempts a more "literary" resolution to the narrative. Since "literary" is a very loaded term I will qualify it in this instance to mean only a structural adjustment to attempt to meet the requirements of a readership with a generally different ideological purview, a purview which itself constructs such categories as literary/nonliterary: the middle class. Note, this does not soften the internal polemic of the story; indeed, it may even sharpen its working-class effect by enunciating the working class as subject with the structural finesse of the bourgeoisie. The second version works because its dialogic sideward glance at the reader interacts well with the context in which it is delivered. Thus, the narrator concludes by recalling the same person he had remembered earlier while in jail. The anecdote about the narrator and Alf as kids constitutes the first narrative event of the narrator's "visions," and their pub scene forms the last moment of the story as a whole. Obviously there are similar narrative subtleties in the earlier version, but here they conveniently allow: (1) the story to finish with the narrator out of jail, and (2) the story to end without direct appeals to socialist inspiration. Both, I believe, allow us to see the importance of the shifting relationships between author, text, and reader—and the relevance of dialogism in understanding them. If sign is the arena of class struggle we should attend to the processes that determine its production and reception.

I stated earlier that working-class fiction is self-conscious of its margina status, and I hope the discussion above has begun to show why. That thi marginalization of voice is staged within the narrative through the doubly marg

nalized articulation of Liza makes this st intent, although we must also say that Sil of discourse in the margins. I should add th implications of dialogism to an understan instance, the dialogic angles that I have dis larger contextual framework (including that less to say, the ideological implications of th broached on this occasion, although they wi section on *Saturday Night and Sunday Morn* hear voices in everything, the dialogism of th (witness the discussion of carnivalization in t of context tells us that we cannot merely dupl least attend to their spirit.

Liza can never quite be what the narrat fortunate as it is inevitable. What I have tried t nature of the sign allows class analysis of langu of the oppressed can be more, or other than clas than that. Yet what Liza's story calls into questi of class struggle as the shifting nature of its relati Dialogism is but one way of describing the soci relations and this is why Liza's voice is always m sion of it including, shall we say, the look in the a this text. Whether in our reading, "Liza" or "Sillit look into each other's eyes in a materialist recogn problem with implications beyond the limits of the which this particular mode of dialogic analysis inex

# 4

# "Once a Rebel":
## *Saturday Night and Sunday Morning*

*Saturday Night and Sunday Morning* is Sillitoe's first published novel and, to date, remains his most significant piece of fiction. Sillitoe had been writing fiction for ten years before that book found a publisher—indeed, from the time he was hospitalized and pensioned out of the military with tuberculosis. He wrote voraciously, struggling to find a voice that would give form to his consciousness. Sillitoe remembers the difficulty of those years: "A pen was my enemy at first: too many gobbled books were pushing my elbow: too many ideas that weren't my own crept in shallow disguise onto the paper: platoons of synonyms and clichés sneaked through defenses that were practically non-existent."[1] Sillitoe's anxiety of influence was conditioned not by his ignorance of literary tradition, but by his fear of it. Much of what he read during those years of convalescence he believed to be inadequate to his vision. Of course, not all of this recognition was his own: indeed, Robert Graves, who was a significant mentor for Sillitoe during his stay in Majorca, had suggested that the man from Nottingham give up trying to write within the grain of the English literary tradition.[2] Sillitoe heeded Graves's advice and decided "to find a line of plain English" with its roots in his own experience.[3]

In what follows I am going to pick up on the theme of dialogism developed in the analysis of Sillitoe's "The Good Women" and explain its importance to our understanding of *Saturday Night and Sunday Morning*. Although Sillitoe would disagree with the term "working class," *Saturday Night and Sunday Morning* is an articulation of the strength and dilemmas of the very possibility of a working-class fiction. It is important to remember that to theorize working-class writing, especially when that writing is a novel, is not intended to prescribe what an ideal version of that writing should be. The dialogism of the oppressed can only be read against a history in which its "dialogic angling" is inscribed and this process should not be idealized as a monument to the class (or race, or gender) from which it is voiced.

The error of "monumentalism" can easily be exampled with regard to the critical reception of *Saturday Night and Sunday Morning*. Because of the author and subject of the novel, categorization is assumed rather than critically examined. For Anthony West, for instance, it is enough that *Saturday Night and Sunday Morning* is a "genuine working-class novel." For Saul Maloff, Sillitoe has clearly "made possible a working-class novel" (although one wonders what Maloff would have made of Greenwood's *Love on the Dole* or Tressell's *The Ragged Trousered Philanthropists*).[4] It is interesting to note Sillitoe's resistance to such labeling: "The greatest inaccuracy was ever to call the book a 'working-class novel' for it is really nothing of the sort. It is simply a novel, and the label given it by most reviewers at the time it came out, even the intelligent ones who should have known better, was simply a way of categorizing a piece of work they weren't capable of assessing from their narrow class standpoint."[5] Monumentalism, when applied to works that do not announce themselves as "traditional," is an ideological marginalization of *les cultures subalternes,* a kind of "if in doubt, dub it proletarian" attitude. Yet Sillitoe's own assessment is not unproblematic, for when has a novel ever been "simply a novel" or a novelist, indeed, simply a novelist. To modify D. H. Lawrence, one can trust neither the artist nor the tale when it comes to literary theory, for the artist, the tale, and the theorist are rarely innocent. In my earlier study of "cultural event" I suggested that the event itself was a form of mediating process, the "unconscious" containment strategy of a culture under threat. Monumentalism speaks through the same ideological determination and seeks to sanitize by default any Habermasian "counter public" challenge to cultural hegemony. Thus my reading of *Saturday Night and Sunday Morning* does not purport to "simply" rename this novel working class, but explain how the work comes to mean in class-specific ways. The dialogism of the oppressed therefore exposes some important implications about working-class writing in general, and the novel in particular.

A consideration of the dialogism of the oppressed with respect to Sillitoe's *Saturday Night and Sunday Morning* requires careful exegesis of Bakhtin's particular claims for dialogism *in the novel.* Later, Sillitoe's text will throw some light on Bakhtin's problematic formulations which will in turn reassert the dialectical nature of this textual analysis. The cornerstone of dialogism is that verbal discourse is a social phenomenon. Once an utterance is extracted from the context in which it is made, its sound dimension is lost; it becomes an abstract specimen codified, for instance, as an individualized stylistic. As Bakhtin notes: "More often than not, stylistics defines itself as a stylistics of 'private craftsmanship' and ignores the social life of discourse outside the artist's study, discourse in the open spaces of public squares, streets, cities and villages, of social groups, generations and epochs."[6] This, Bakhtin maintains, misses the point when applied to the novel:

The novel as a whole is a phenomenon multiform in style and variform in speech and tone. In it the investigator is confronted with several heterogeneous stylistic unities, often located on different linguistic levels and subject to different stylistic controls. The stylistic uniqueness of the novel as a genre consists precisely in the combination of these subordinate yet still relatively autonomous unities (even at times comprised of different languages) into the higher unity of the work as a whole: the style of a novel is to be found in the combination of its styles; the language of a novel is the system of its "languages."[7]

Just as Bakhtin's theory of sign is useful in the analysis of working-class language, so his comprehension of the novel helps to build a conceptual framework for understanding working-class writing. First, the novel is indeed a system of languages, to ascribe the whole as working-class utterance would be to monologize its dialogicity, its many-voicedness. Second, although the languages of the novel cannot all be working-class, the way these unities are *combined* may well constitute the mark of what we can call a working-class stylistics (in other words, a *social* rather than an individualized stylistics). Pierre Bourdieu, for instance, has suggested that it is only in language that working-class practice achieves stylization: here it is the language juxtaposition of the novel that implicates this counter-cultural practice.[8] The problem with Bakhtin's theory for our purposes is that the stylistic unities of which he writes are subordinated to what he believes to be the organic stylistic whole of the novel. It may well be that the sum of novelistic style is more than its component stylistics, but to posit this as an organic whole lends itself to more traditional valorization of the novel as form.[9] That the novel orchestrates a social diversity of speech types is crucial to our analysis; however, Bakhtin's claims for the "higher unity" of the novel have political repercussions that will be addressed later. For now, let me reiterate that a working-class novel is distinguished not by a totality of working-class language, but by how the language styles of its narrative are articulated together. If we propose that Alan Sillitoe writes a working-class novel in *Saturday Night and Sunday Morning,* it is not because this novel can be reduced to single class utterance, but because of the *way* he juxtaposes different language styles within one and the same work. All writers have heteroglossia available to them, yet the way they select can be differentiated according to varied social purviews—purviews that are mediated and over-determined by class. It is important to note that this process of selection is not the product of authorial intent, as Bakhtin points out:

The phenomenon usually called "creative individuality" is, in fact, the expression of a firm and constant line of social focus (orientation), i.e. the expression of class views, class sympathies and antipathies of the particular person as they have been laid down and shaped in the material of his internal speech. The sociologycal [*sic*] structure of inner speech at its upper layer, and its inbuilt *social orientations,* to a great extent predetermine the ideological and, in particular the artistic creation of the given individual and in such creation come to their ultimate development and finalization.[10]

Class here becomes indelibly inscribed as the inner speech or consciousness of an individual. Thus, inner speech is the product of social interrelationships— of social being. In Bakhtin this is a precondition to outer or "external literary speech." The movement from inner expression to outer utterance is the first stage of literary "creation." The second stage of the process requires an orientation or recognition of a projected listener or reader. The final stage of artistic realization is what Bakhtin calls a "technical rearrangement of the material" that takes account of editor, publisher, printer, and markets.[11] The way that language styles are juxtaposed in the working-class novel is thus the process identified as the second stage of Bakhtin's theoretical apparatus, inextricably linked as it is to both the first and third. It is using the second stage that I will begin to examine the dialogic processes that mediate *Saturday Night and Sunday Morning* as a working-class novel. A brief focus, however, on the first stage of the artistic process, the determinations of inner speech will serve as a backdrop to the analysis of language/style juxtaposition in *Saturday Night and Sunday Morning*.

Sillitoe spent most of his first twenty years in Nottingham in poverty and distress. Later he would recall the harsh six years when his father was unemployed and meat was a luxury item that appeared only on Sundays.[12] When Sillitoe entered the Raleigh bicycle factory at fourteen, his formal education came to an end, but the industrial experience would not be lost on him. Such biographical details are only useful to the extent that they help to indicate the social orientation of the artist. In *Raw Material,* Sillitoe's book of concrete experiences measured by an abstract meditation on truth, Sillitoe had ample opportunity to imagine himself free from the orientation forged in his youth— yet the book reads as a curious tribute to those years, a recognition that the social milieu of a successful artist can not erase the past, but throws it into relief.[13] Sillitoe's creative character is not formed in spite of his working-class background, but through it. Through this the comprehension of the writer in relation to the reader is established. As Bakhtin asserts:

> It is here that their common language is worked out and their interrelationship (or, more precisely, their mutual orientation). Both author and reader meet on common non-literary ground, perhaps they work at the same place, they may take part in the same meetings and assemblies, chat over tea, listen to the same conversations, read the same newspapers and books, go to the same films. This, then, is where their "inner worlds" are built up, given shape, and standardized. In other words there is a kind of special "hybridization" between their views and opinions, a kind of hybridization of the inner language of the whole group of people.[14]

A central dilemma is posed here that Bakhtin's essay does not help to elucidate. The working-class writer often writes outside of the workplace and social environment that determines working-class consciousness. It is not that the writer cannot recreate this relationship in the imagination, but that the worker who earns a living from writing inexorably becomes severed from the milieu that informs that consciousness. Since such statements about class consciousness and literary production are often taken as a resuscitation of reflectionism more should be said about the contradictory consciousness of the working-class writer. Consciousness is not seen here as the unmediated product of particular social relations; rather, it is precisely the fact that consciousness is constantly overdetermined by ideological effects that literary representation is here read through Bakhtin's discursive categorization. Gayatri Spivak's thoughtful essay "Subaltern Studies: Deconstructing Historiography" provides some crucial insight into the tracing of subaltern consciousness that has some important implications for the current argument.

> I am progressively inclined . . . to read the retrieval of subaltern consciousness as the charting of what in post-structuralist language would be called the subaltern subject-effect. A subject–effect can be briefly plotted as follows: that which seems to operate as a subject may be part of an immense discontinous network ("text" in the general sense) of strands that may be termed politics, ideology, economics, history, sexuality, language. (Each of these strands, if they are isolated, can also be seen as woven of many strands.) . . . Yet the continuist and homogenist deliberative consciousness symptomatically requires a continuous and homogenous cause for this effect and thus posits a sovereign and determining subject. This latter is, then, the effect of an effect, and its positing a metalepsis, or the substitution of an effect for a cause.[15]

Spivak's counter to reflectionist theories of subjectivity and consciousness is to argue for the overdetermination of subject effects, which may sound like a theoretical oxymoron, yet nevertheless avoids the simplistic equation of determinate causes with probable effects. Bakhtin's theory of dialogism is similar in this regard for class subjectivity never resides in some metaphysical subject position but is instead bound up in the continual dialogic relations between subjects. This is what we might call the textual terrain of subject effects, the space of subaltern consciousness; in this case, the consciousness of the working-class writer. Sillitoe's career cannot simply be summed up as the exploration of this space but, I would argue, he has written his most significant works precisely at that point where his literary skills attempt to envoice subaltern subject effects, the raw material of his inner speech. Again, this is not some plea for class as a mirroring of the real in language, but for analysis of class discourse as a particular refraction of social relations with all the concomitant contradictions that that may imply.

The approach sketched above does not offer the prospect of a more or less homogenous set of works whose characteristics can be made the hallmarks of some alternative tradition, partly because the politics of reading often put such writings under erasure, but more specifically because the writing itself is often complicit with its own negation. The subaltern writer in the social margins of discursive practice may introject precisely that hegemonic ideology and consciousness that marginalizes her or him producing, for instance, working-class fiction that doubts its own specificity, its own voice and audience. The hybridization of which Bakhtin writes indeed embodies a curious negative capability.

As my discussion of "The Good Women" has indicated, who the writer writes for is problematic, a difficulty marked by dialogic angling in response to utterance context. Hybridization needs to be considered dialogically if we are to understand the languages that run counter to a writer's "basic social orientation" yet nevertheless find a place in the utterances of a writer's work. This difficulty is especially problematic in the case of working-class fiction because of a critical tendency to dismiss the possibility of a working-class audience.

For instance, in the sixties Stephen Spender maintained that there was no "working-class audience for novels by working-class writers about the working class."[16] Sillitoe, he contends, writes for a middle-class public: "The idea of the working-class point of view in fiction was a love affair of youth. The writer has to settle down, alas, to marriage with the middle-class reader."[17] It is a problem that Sillitoe had obviously considered himself: "Though proletarian novelists are read mostly by a middle-class audience they should make themselves readable by the people they grew up with—not necessarily an impediment to good writing."[18] He adds, "Factory workers enjoy reading about their own environment, and few books will allow them to do this."[19] On another occasion Sillitoe notes, "Working men and women who read do not have the privilege of seeing themselves honestly and realistically portrayed in novels."[20] Sillitoe has been as insistent about writing for the working class as he has been about denying evaluations of him as a working-class writer. *Saturday Night and Sunday Morning,* at least, gives credence to the former view over the latter.

The main character of *Saturday Night and Sunday Morning* is Arthur Seaton, a rugged lad of twenty-one who works at the Raleigh bicycle factory in Nottingham. As in "The Good Women," the narrative is constructed through the depiction of a milieu. This is achieved not just by description of a working-class environment (although there is enough of that to recreate proletarian life in postwar Nottingham), but by the language employed. The book begins at an incredible pace, evocative of Arthur's frantic Saturday nights: the reader is pitched headlong into Arthur's world much like Arthur falling down stairs in the first few lines. Just like Jimmy Porter in *Look Back in Anger,* Arthur's introduction is a loud riposte to the quietude of British fiction of the 1950s. Not only is the pace of the narrative adequate to its description, but the language is full of "markers" that are culturally specific to the British working class.

It was Benefit Night for the White Horse Club, and the pub had burst its contribution box and spread a riot through its rooms and between its four walls. Floors shook and windows rattled, and leaves of aspidistras wilted in the fumes of beer and smoke. Notts County had beaten the visiting team, and the members of the White Home supporters club were quartered upstairs to receive a flow of victory. Arthur was not a member of the club, but Brenda was, and so he was drinking the share of her absent husband—as far as it would go, and when the club went bust and the shrewd publican put on the towels for those that couldn't pay, he laid eight half-crowns on the table, intending to fork out for his own.

For it was Saturday night, the best and bingiest glad-time of the week, one of the fifty-two holidays in the slow turning Big Wheel of the year, a violent preamble to a prostrate Sabbath. Piled up passions were exploded on Saturday night, and the effect of a week's monotonous graft in the factory was swilled out of your system in a burst of good will. You followed the motto of "be drunk and be happy," kept your crafty arms around female waists, and felt the beer going beneficially down into the elastic capacity of your guts.[21]

Obviously, English working-class culture is more than what is depicted here: it is more than the realism that conveys a sense of a working-class milieu. Yet it seems to me that there can be no theory of working class culture if we cannot account for the importance of such passages within that broader culture. The first point is that the event should not be interpreted as typical, for this assessment only supports debilitating stereotypes of working-class men as beer-swilling animals. This is a key criticism of Ronald D. Vaverka's analysis of *Saturday Night and Sunday Morning* and cannot be overstressed.[22] Any criticism that takes a working-class individual to represent the working class, rather than as an individual among other members of that class is objectifying in a politically reactionary way.[23]

The markers that I mentioned are the historically specific cultural signifiers of class. The pub as meeting place is as familiar to readers of Lawrence's *Sons and Lovers* as the aspidistras to readers of Orwell. The importance of the local football team needs no further mention except as a reminder that many professional football clubs in England began as workers' sports clubs within industrial firms. We should note at this point that the markers are specifically those of the working-class male, although this presentation is by no means consistent and unchallenged throughout the book—a subject to which I will return.[24]

The first part of the above quoation, despite the markers of working-class culture, is written in standard English: there is neither the Queen's English tone of the British bourgeoisie—nor any slang or use of dialect usually associated with the representation of the lower orders (much like Shakespeare's ideological division of poetry and prose in his plays). Yet in the second paragraph the language shifts gear—and quite clearly articulates that sideward glance that is the hallmark of double-voiced discourse. In this particular example, the effect is achieved in two ways. First, there is a shift in phrasing. "Bingiest glad-time," is a good description of pub consumption on a Saturday night, and is not usually associated with cocktail parties. Sabbath might also be a day of rest for the middle class, but it is rarely described as "prostrate." Similarly, passions may build, but for the worker who fills a pallet with a thousand pieces of drilled and burred metal every day, passions "pile up" too. Finally, although this has a regional as well as class evocation, arms are never sly or wily: they are "crafty." On most occasions we will see that it is not the words themselves that are working class (for as Bakhtin states, "words are neutral") but their specific combination within a complex cultural context.

The second class-specific dialogization of language is conveyed through the shift of narrative position. The more colloquial the language, the more the narrative is driven by direct address—the use of "you." In *Saturday Night and Sunday Morning* this regularly signifies an approximation to Arthur's thoughts as Arthur would express them, or what Bakhtin calls "the stylistically individualized speech of character." In addition, the use of "you" is a direct reader appeal that can underline an identification between the narrative and its reader. Thus the motto, "be drunk and be happy" is the mark of that incessant motto maker, Arthur himself. This sort of identification Sillitoe believed was important, but it can also be read as a source of alienation either within the working class or in opposition to other class cultures; quite simply "you" cannot always identify with the beneficial nature of beer going down into "the elastic capacity of *your* guts." Sillitoe shifts language styles, consciously or not, according to the perspective in which Arthur can best be communicated—for Arthur is the central character of the story and in altering the relative position of the reader in relation to the represented consciousness of Arthur, this character becomes the central challenge of the book. To accept Arthur as he is, is to accept a drunken lout whose solidarity for his fellow male workers extends to sleeping with their wives while the men are on the night shift. Yet to accept this is also to recognize that Arthur's individual morality has wider repercussions and that his fiercely antiestablishment rhetoric issues from the same sensibility. Although his sensibility is not typical of the working class as a whole (which would be the mistake of stereotypic objectification), the language shifts and markers are certainly indicative of a class position.

One last point on this passage. That Saturday is a festive occasion, "one of the fifty-two holidays in the slow-turning Big Wheel of the year," is clearly portrayed as welcome relief from "the monotonous graft [work] in the factory." The carousing is a "glad-time" interlude before resuming work on the line and, although this is not an apology for "binging," anybody who has worked on a shop floor will understand the sentiments and importance of letting go on a Saturday night. True to the Bakhtinian "belly laughter" one can associate with this pub scene, Arthur falls down the stairs, then vomits over a man, then a woman. The temptation here is to impute some sense of "carnivalesque." The pub, however, is a world unto itself and rarely stages the topsy-turvy characteristics of carnival (unlike Goose Fair later in the book).[25] True, the scene itself can be read as a carnivalizing of novelistic convention, since the majority of English novels do not feature this form of cultural arena. But the working-class effects here are achieved through language stylistics rather than just through content components.

A working-class novel can be working class because it expresses the workers' position in the production and reproduction of social relations.[26] To this end, such a novel must not only show workers in relation to each other outside the workplace, but must represent them as part of the productive process—for it is clearly a different novel that effaces the activity of production, as the activity of producers, from its pages.[27] Furthermore, the nature of work should be seen as integral rather than coincidental to the progression of the narrative. Thus, many novels may have working-class effects, but few can be considered working class if they do not attempt to represent the fundamental aspect of the working class—the relations associated with the sale of its labor in order to subsist. It cannot be denied that working-class existence is more than working in this job or that, but to produce fiction that simply ignores this facet of working-class existence is to ignore the class character of social formation. There are other criteria that can be discussed,[28] but at this point I want to look at how Sillitoe's language mediates the role of work in Arthur's existence. To what extent, therefore, are we presented working-class labor as Arthur experiences it?

> Arthur reached his capstan lathe and took off his jacket, hanging it on a near-by nail so that he could keep an eye on his belongings. He pressed the starter button, and his motor came to life with a gentle thump. Looking around, it did not seem, despite the infernal noise of hurrying machinery, that anyone was working with particular speed. He smiled to himself and picked up a glittering steel cylinder from the top box of a pile beside him, and fixed it into the spindle. He jettisoned his cigarette into the sud-pan, drew back the capstan, and swung back the turret on to its broadest drill. Two minutes passed while he contemplated the precise position of tools and cylinder; finally he spat onto both hands and rubbed them together, then switched on the sud-tap in front of the movable brass pipe, pressed a button that set the spindle running, and ran in the drill to a neat chamfer. Monday morning had lost its terror.[29]

David Craig has said of this description that it is "the first passage I know of in our literature (nearly two centuries after the first power-loom was patented!) which evokes a factory worker's experiences from the inside with the finesse that writers have given to all the others in the human range."[30] Nigel Gray's reaction is a little more traditional: "You can get used to anything. But this sort of environment cannot help but curb your sensitivity, deaden your feelings, limit your awareness."[31] Such comments are, of course, useful in an assessment of Sillitoe's oeuvre, although they need a firmer theoretical underpinning to gauge the "working classness" of his writing. Surely what is important here is not just that we have a description of a worker in a working environment, but that Sillitoe is evoking Arthur's *relationship* to that environment in terms that go beyond the "alienated worker" stereotype. The best description in this writing does not try to reproduce some principles of social analysis (which was the mistake of socialist realism in the thirties), but is itself a measure of how to formulate these principles. This passage is significant because it shows the worker as a producer and as a thinking part of the productive process. Arthur, unlike many stereotypes of the working class, does not live in spite of his work, he lives through it. This does not mean that Arthur necessarily likes it, nor indeed that he is not alienated from the means and ends of production. What I mean here is that the relationship between worker and machine is fully articulated as part of a broader way of living: work is not merely tangential to living.

In this example the language is marked by its ordinariness: there is no attempt to embellish the description of work. In effect, the passage proceeds as a meticulous observation of the necessary components for Arthur's act of work. Yet the simple language does not preclude what I have earlier referred to, using Bakhtin, as "internal polemic."[32] The sideward glance of this passage is unspoken, and rests in Arthur's smiling to himself. The workers do not seem to be working with particular speed because few of them are actually working. Like Arthur, they take these few minutes on Monday morning to make their personal adjustments to the task ahead. Unlike the machines, they cannot be turned on and off. Arthur's smile is an indication that he knows he works the machine and not the other way around, and that these moments of contemplation are resistance rituals (like absenteeism and pilfering) that clearly define Arthur's interests in opposition to those who believe they control him.[33] The language, therefore, does not mystify this ritual, but highlights it precisely by the understated delivery. Instead of *introjecting* in the Lukacsian sense, the experience of work and thereby becoming unconsciously compliant with the forces of domination over workers—the way Arthur brushes off the terror of Monday morning—"internally distantiates" the ideology of complicity. He cannot escape the relations of production, at least not on an individual level, but he is not merely a function of them either. To this extent, Sillitoe's own experience of the production line was not wasted on him.

The working-class language of *Saturday Night and Sunday Morning* has, of course, a political orientation. Again, this is rarely because bold-faced political statements are placed in Arthur's mouth, but because of the way his class position is articulated. His personal politics are not seen to be those of an ideal socialist, as if this were the natural disposition of a worker. But neither does Arthur believe that the inequalities he sees and experiences are merely to be blithely accepted. Arthur's politics are contradictory and move quickly from conviction to resignation to conviction again. What is interesting is that Arthur's ruminations on politics are strongly individualistic, as if he believes on occasion that there is no communal interest with which he can identify. In passage after passage the language enunciates quick shifts in political affiliation as Arthur articulates his version of "Us and Them."[34]

I've 'eard that blokes as win football pools get thousands o' beggin' letters, but yer know what I'd do if I got 'em? I'll tell yer what I'd do: I'd mek a bonfire on 'em. Because I don't believe in share and share alike, Jack. Tek them blokes as spout on boxes outside the factory sometimes. I like to hear 'em talk about Russia, about farms and power stations they've got, because it's interestin', but when they say that when they get in government everybody's got to share and share alike, then that's another thing. I ain't a communist, I tell you. I like 'em though because they're different from those big fat Tory bastards in parliament. And them Labour bleeders too.[35]

Or later:

Cunning, he told himself gleefully, as he began the first hundred, dropping them off one by one at a respectable speed. Don't let the bastards grind you down, as Fred used to say when he was in the navy. . . . I'll never let anybody grind me down because I'm worth as much as any other man in the world, though when it comes to the lousy vote they give me I often feel like telling 'em where to shove it. For all the good using it'll do me. But if they said: "Look, Arthur, here's a hundred-weight of dynamite and a brand new plunger, now blow up the factory," then I'd do it, because that'd be something worth doing. Action. I'd bale out for Russia or the North Pole where I'd sit and laugh like a horse over what I'd done, at the wonderful sight of gaffers and machines and shining bikes going sky high one wonderful moonlit night. Not that I've got owt against 'em, but that's just how I feel now and again. Me, I couldn't care less if the world did blow up tomorrow, as long as I'm blown up with it. Not that I wouldn't like to win ninety-thousand grand beforehand. But I'm having a good life and don't care about anything, and it'd be a pity to leave Brenda, all said and done, especially now Jack's been put on nights. Not that he minds, which is the funny part about it, because he's happy about a bigger pay packet and a change, and I'm happy, and I know Brenda's happy. Everybody's happy. It's a fine world sometimes, if you don't weaken, or if you don't give the bastards a chance to get cracking with that carborundum.[36]

These examples are worth quoting at length not because of the stream-of-consciousness technique employed, although that in itself is notable, but because of, for instance, the shift to the first person when a political position is being articulated (including the shifts from one politics to another within that discourse), and the fact that the vacillation itself suggests yet another overall political purview. In part the passages proceed according to what Bakhtin identifies as "vari-directional double-voiced discourse."[37] Arthur's statements are overdetermined by what we have learned of him through the language stratification in other parts of the book. The fact that here Arthur's thoughts are presented in the first person tends to parodically represent his position. The parody distances rather than encourages identification through the use of first-person narration, hence the vari-directional quality. In effect, Arthur's first-person narration is continually marked by ambivalence. Arthur says he does not believe in share and share alike, but then says he likes the communists; at another moment he admits to voting communist, then adds that it was not because he liked them, but because he wanted to back the underdog. If his selfish individualism is quite in keeping with Tory ideology, he yet voices nothing but contempt for it. On this point, perhaps Hoggart's fear of "working class hedonism" was over-stressed. Like Arthur, Arthur Machin, Joe Lampton, Billy Liar, and, of course, Jimmy Porter have few natural predilections for the Right Wing—yet part of their dilemma is a distrust for a Left in Britain that has not been responsible for their "affluence."[38]

Arthur's chief motto is uttered several times through the text—"Don't let the bastards grind you down" (*nil illegitimi carborundum*—hence Arthur's reference to the carborundum wheel that is used to sharpen tools in the factory). "Bastards" covers many groups within the narrative, but collectively they constitute "Them": Tories, bosses or gaffers, military chiefs (Arthur learns this from a brief period in the army), foremen, government, anybody or anything in a position of authority over Arthur. As for one person/one vote, Arthur well understands what kind of democratic equality that has led to. He therefore considers "action," in this case blowing up the factory and the gaffer. But such revolutionary consciousness is quickly undermined: he does not have "owt against 'em," it is just a feeling he gets from time to time. And disarmament? Well, so what if the whole world blows up says Arthur. Communism to socialism to anarchism to nihilism: Arthur runs a gamut of political affiliation in sentence after sentence. He is consistently against the Tories but in opposition he becomes just as consistently against everything else. No belief is prioritized, none remains unchallenged or contradicted. That this is parodied becomes obvious when Arthur, after all this invective, notes that he is having a good life and does not care about anything. If he does not care, we might ask, then why does he get so upset when considering "Them"? And if he does not care about anything why, in the next sentence, does he care about Brenda? Everybody is happy, but everyone is certainly not. This parodic distance, underlined as it is by the use of the first-person narration (in a text that is predominantly written in the third person) is not intended to mock in the strong sense of the word, but shows that Arthur's class position in no way automatically produces the "correct" political apprehension of it. Social being indeed determines consciousness, but political alliance is contingent on many variables at any one moment in history. If the working-class youth of England in the 1950s were disaffected from "Tory socialism" this did not lead them inexorably into any particular radical politics above all others. That Sillitoe does not put any more than this into the main character of *Saturday Night and Sunday Morning* shows more social perspicacity than wish fulfillment, but it is a purview mediated by Sillitoe's own peculiar relationship to English politics during the period. In this light Craig and Egan are right to argue for the articulation of literature as "evidence"[39] or, in this interpretation, literary production as itself a symptomatic "reading" of historical determination.[40]

The use of "I" in *Saturday Night and Sunday Morning* therefore, often displaces political purview across a wide range of possible positions. I have mentioned the use of "you" earlier as a dialogic shift of language stylistic, but in this context I want to indicate that this form of direct address is employed to represent Arthur's most coherent political "voice." Given the above, it might seem that the use of the second person is a discrete form of monologization that imputes a semantic authority to Arthur's political position that is not evident in the first-person narration. There is enough to suggest, however, that despite the coherence in the "you" narration, it does not contradict the overall political rhetoric of the book; if anything, it empowers it. Arthur believes in this, that, and the other, but when belief is presented through the second person a dialogic sideward glance is involved—if *you* experience the world in similar ways to Arthur what do *you* believe in? Dialogic narration asks the reader to identify with the discourse. To the working-class writer such sideward glances are addressed to a working-class reader and, although they can be appreciated by other readers with different social purviews, such communication is as culturally specific as any other communication. The working-class effect of such address is not to be found in the mere disagreement of "speaker" and "listener," but in the communal understanding it generates between differentiated and individualized members of a group situated by their role in the production and reproduction of social relations. Class is an abstract term, but experience of class is actually, however individualized, quite concrete.

> Once a rebel, always a rebel. You can't help being one. You can't deny that. And it's best to be a rebel so as to show 'em it don't pay to try to do you down. Factories and labour exchanges and insurance officers keep us alive and kicking—so they say—but they're booby traps and will suck you under like sinking sands if you aren't careful. Factories sweat you to death, labour exchanges talk you to death, insurance and income tax officers milk money from your wage packets and rob you to death. And if you're still left with a tiny bit of life in your guts after all this boggering about, the army calls you up and you get shot to death. And if you're clever enough to stay out of the army you get bombed to death. Ay, by God, it's a hard life if you don't weaken, if you don't stop that bastard government from grinding your face in the muck, though there ain't much you can do about it unless you start making dynamite to blow their four-eyed clocks to bits.
>
> They shout at you from soapboxes: "Vote for me, and this and that," but it amounts to the same in the end whatever you vote for because it means a government that puts stamps all over your phizzog until you can't see a hand before you, and what's more makes you buy 'em so's they can keep on doing it. They've got you by the guts, by backbone and skull, until they think you'll come whenever they whistle.
>
> But listen, this lathe is my everlasting pal because it gets me thinking, and that's their big mistake because I know I'm not the only one. One day they'll bark and we won't run into a pen like sheep.[41]

There are many elements here that recall the invective of the earlier examples: yet on this occasion they do not contradict each other; each view complements the next. There is again the opposition to the factories, the government, the military, and the suspicion of certain political beliefs delivered from soap-boxes. There is again the motto about not letting the bastards grind you down, and the possibility that dynamite is one response to the oppression that you feel. In the first two paragraphs of this passage there is an overwhelming sense of entrapment, which concretely justifies the ideology of rebellion, "You can't help being one. You can't deny that." For those who are not enmeshed in such social relations, these statements do not offer identification, but alienation. Nonetheless, the position espoused does not appear out of the air: the social situation from which this view emanates is textually consistent and specific to the text in history. Thus, on this occasion, when the narrative switches back from second person to first person the discourse is not parodic, but polemical. Furthermore, it is noticeable that although Arthur speaks as an individual, he enunciates a communal interest whose appeal he feels goes beyond his personal politics, "One day they'll bark and we won't run into a pen like sheep." For working-class readers this can be read as an expression of solidarity, for some other readers this can only be read as a threat.

There are many themes that I have not discussed in relation to *Saturday Night and Sunday Morning:* the comedy, for instance: the mouse at the factory, "shooting" Mrs. Bull the gossip, and rolling the drunk's car would all be significant components of an analysis of the humor of the work, again with attendant class effects. More detailed descriptive analysis could be made of the contemporary culture portrayed in the book including those elements that Hoggart labels as "demons"—newspapers, television, and the cinema. What I have tried to emphasize, however, is that an understanding of the class specificity of *Saturday Night and Sunday Morning* is primarily to be found in its language. The language of *Saturday Night and Sunday Morning* rarely attempts to "normalize" according to an acceptable or codified novelistic discourse. Many novels also do this, of course, one only has to think of the work of Joyce. What is interesting here, however, is that the linguistic deviations, or what Bakhtin calls, "the centrifugal forces of language" are given a specific social orientation that counters the centripetal tendencies of a "unitary language." In *Saturday Night and Sunday Morning* I have taken the centrifugal forces to be those which are broadly working class. The centripetal forces of the life of language, embodied in a "unitary language," operate in the midst of heteroglossia. At any given moment of its evolution, language is stratified not only into linguistic dialectic in the strict sense of the word (according to formal linguistic markers, especially phonetic), but also (and for us this is the essential point) into languages that are socio-ideological: languages of social groups, "professional" and "generic languages," languages of generations and so forth.[42] The relationship between these two tendencies of centripetal and centrifugal forces is one of struggle, a struggle where dialogic language contests the centralization of culture at any one moment in history. So far I have demonstrated these shifting relations of languages across complete utterances through *Saturday Night and Sunday Morning*. But since class struggle intersects in sign, it follows that the dialogism of the oppressed cannot only be tracked across utterances, but also across a single word.

One of the central events of *Saturday Night and Sunday Morning* is Brenda's pregnancy and the subsequent abortion. Like many other "episodes" in the book, this was originally the theme of a short story which underlines its relative importance to Sillitoe, despite the fact that many critics to date have overlooked the centrality of Arthur's relationship with Brenda and this scene in particular in terms of the novel as a whole.[43] Yet unwanted pregnancy itself is a significant *topos* of working-class fiction, in no small measure because it is a fact of working-class existence. Obviously, it occurs outside the working class, but in different societies, at different times, it becomes a particular problem of the working class because of their economic position vis-à-vis other social groups. Abortion becomes still more distressing if no relatively safe means are within the economic reach of working-class women who choose to terminate their pregnancy.

Mary Eagleton and David Pierce have already noted how the theme of abortion runs through working-class fiction in the period under discussion, including Delaney's *A Taste of Honey*, Dunn's *Up the Junction*, Hines's *The Blinder* and Braine's *Room at the Top*.[44] All of this work shows how abortion is not only gender-specific, but is complicated by class considerations.[45] Money in *The Blinder* reduces the problem of what to do, but lack of it in *A Taste of Honey* undermines choice. That the semantic orientation of abortion is determined by its social context is highly relevant to our analysis of dialogism in Sillitoe's writing. Moreover, abortion's significant presence as a social act within *Saturday Night and Sunday Morning* is marked by its significant absence as a word. When considering abortion, therefore, we must evaluate its dialogic suppression in the languages of class.

The word "appears" in the text as a series of euphemisms, phrases designed to give cultural expression to a social taboo. Both Arthur and Brenda talk of "getting rid of it" (p. 61) but later, on his own, Arthur provides a veritable compendium of uttering the unutterable: "Who would have thought it? Brenda on the tub, up the stick, with a bun in the oven, and now he had to pump Aunt Ada and find out how to empty the tub, throw Brenda to the bottom of the stick, and sling that half cooked bun from the stoked-up oven" (p. 62). With an acumen typical of his masculinist bravado, Arthur puts every name he can to what must happen except the one that is its most powerful signifier. Of course, one could argue that such a word is not part of Arthur's vocabulary, but then one still has to consider the sociocultural reasons why this is so. For instance, the repression of the word itself is obviously bound by a form of masculine guilt. Indeed, the word's absent presence is powerful enough to produce Arthur's sense of absent cause, "How do you know its mine?" he accuses Brenda (p. 60). And again later, to his Aunt Ada, "It's a mate o'mine at work. You see, he's got a young woman into trouble, and he don't know what to do either. So I thought I'd come and see you" (p. 67). Despite denying both word and deed, Arthur does seek communal help for a problem that has no easy economic solution. In this way, the absence of alternatives determines a community response which provides both a solution and a metalanguage for a word that does not appear in the work.

The ceremony of "bringing it off," as it is called, is described in detail in the book. Brenda sits in a bath of near boiling water, drinking gin until she is senseless. Arthur is with her, so is one "half-touched" friend, Em'ler, who has been convinced that the unwanted child has been the doing of Brenda's husband, Jack. Arthur waits for the gin to "do the trick" and Em'ler keeps Brenda well supplied with gin and hot water until she is sure that "we've brought it off." Brenda collapses into bed and Arthur leaves without being seen by the returning Jack. Finally, in an act that compounds our sense of Arthur's insensitivity, Arthur meets up with Brenda's sister, Winnie, and stays the night with her.

My point here is not to suggest that merely by inserting the word "abortion" into this narrative the event would lose its working-class effect. What I am suggesting is that the absence of the word is conditioned first by its taboo social status, but then secondly by a dialogic overdetermination. That is, the way its absence is achieved is conditioned by a particular social purview. Although silence is mentioned in Bakhtin's oeuvre, it is not articulated as an absent presence, but as "the pause and beginning of the word."[46] To adequately explain the absent word, however, we need to understand how it is exorcised from particular class positions. In this light, it is interesting to note that in the film version of *Saturday Night and Sunday Morning,* which I will be discussing in detail in the next chapter, not only is the act cut from view, but all the class euphemisms are also placed under erasure. The British Board of Film Censors understands perfectly that the word is a site of class struggle; its response is: ~~abortion~~. Their reactionary political position dictates that gin and hot water remedies for a lack of affordable health care should not be represented on the screen. Furthermore, they suggested at the time that the remedy should not succeed unless ambiguously so. If male authorial ideology determines a certain hesitancy regarding the use of "abortion" to describe abortion, then this should not cloud the fact that the politics of naming is also dialogically determined by class, whose ability to give voice to silence is only matched by its attempt to silence voices.

*Saturday Night and Sunday Morning* is a novel, albeit an episodic one as several critics have already pointed out.[47] Since the problem of the novel as form for a working-class writer is to be dealt with later, I will restrict myself here to some concluding remarks on dialogized discourse in the novel. In *Saturday Night and Sunday Morning* Sillitoe combines and juxtaposes several languages to tell his story. I have argued that these combinations are specifically angled by a particular social purview, and that it is this that necessitates its evaluation as a component of a more broadly based working-class culture. The error in Bakhtin's theoretical project, if not in his political purview, is that dialogism in the novel is clearly made to carry too much weight. Does the synthesis of language stratification in the novel mean that other instances of cultural synthesis are of secondary consideration? Both in *The Dialogic Imagination* and *Problems of Dostoevsky's Poetics* there is a danger of fetishizing the novel as form by making it the quintessence of dialogized discourse. Of course, this act can be read historically as a recuperative attempt to offset the poetic preoccupations of the Russian Formalists, but in another context (contemporary criticism, for instance) the primacy of dialogism in the novel can idealize the novel as form over others. The novelization of discourse that Bakhtin identifies as a historical process is an important way of showing the development of prose forms into the twentieth century.[48] But the arguments that Bakhtin made for dialogism in Dostoevsky's novels cannot be assumed to be addressed from the same problematic of form faced by Western academies in the late twentieth century. The forces that open novelistic discourse to people of Sillitoe's social purview can also be those that precisely limit their artistic expression.

For now, I hope that my analysis of dialogism across forms (the short story, the novel, and next in the film) shows the potential for concrete analysis of cultural production informed by, and productive of, a specifically class-oriented purview. Such work begins to pinpoint the shortcomings of conventional genre categorizations of, for instance, the working-class novel. A lot of people "heard" Arthur's voice when *Saturday Night and Sunday Morning* was first published, although many simply did not know what they were hearing—for this is how the "other" is often constructed and marginalized in the same act of consumption. As Raymond Williams has remarked, this was almost bound to be the case: "The simplest descriptive novel about working-class life is already, by being written, a significant and positive cultural intervention. For it is not even yet what a novel is supposed to be, even as one kind amongst others. and changing this takes time."[49] Bakhtin's theory is important in addressing this challenge because the lesson of dialogism is that signs of struggle are struggles over the sign.

# 5

# Projecting the Working Class:
## *Saturday Night and Sunday Morning*, the Film

Alan Sillitoe's literary success was initially guaranteed by two awards: the first for *Saturday Night and Sunday Morning*, which received the Author's Club Award for the best English first novel of 1958; the second for *The Loneliness of the Long Distance Runner* which won the Hawthornden Prize of 1959 for the best prose work of imagination. As I have previously indicated, part of this recognition was conditioned by the cultural event in which these works became inscribed—forces of production and reception that add up to much more than authorial intent. Yet *Saturday Night and Sunday Morning* was not an immediate *popular* success. Of course, among the great works of the Western literary tradition, popularity is not necessarily of prime critical importance. Working-class fiction, however, lives and dies by its popular appeal. As a cultural category, working-class fiction is "produced" not only by the critical act, and the institutions in which that act is justified, but is overdetermined by the readership of a large and literate cultural community, the working class itself. A work of fiction is working-class not only because of its subject and ostensible author, but because it enters into a dialogue with the very interlocutors of which it speaks. Bourgeois books can be read by proletarians, and *proletkult* can be consumed by the bourgeoisie, but working-class fiction without a working-class readership simply cannot exist.[1]

From the above it follows that the working-class effects of the fiction under discussion depend, to a large degree, on the distributive medium of such fiction. As Ken Worpole has discussed in *Reading by Numbers*, our understanding of popular fiction must be informed by analysis of the channels of cultural production and distribution at any one moment in history.[2] Thus, such factors as availability and affordability become important in an assessment of working-class fiction, for these help to determine a readership which is itself a constitutive guarantee of the identity and difference of this culture.

Since I have discussed the publication and initial reception of *Saturday Night and Sunday Morning* earlier I should say that my interest here is with a particular example of its readership fortunes. With all the critical accolades and association with other works of the "Angry Young Men" as cultural event, Sillitoe's "most successful" novel sold eight thousand copies in hardback during its first two years of publication.[3] This was not bad for a first novel in England at the time, yet what many reviewers dubbed a "genuine working-class novel" was not being read primarily by the English working class. Both the price and availability of the novel precluded wide working-class readership. Of the one-sixth of the working class who borrowed at least one book a week from the local library few would have found this book on the shelves, since there were so few copies to go around. When Sillitoe was asked later about the success of *Saturday Night and Sunday Morning* he suggests that its appeal was precisely based on a working-class readership:

> I can only assume that, up to that point, there wasn't such an amount of stuff that somebody, say, like Arthur Seaton could pick up and in which he could read about the sort of life he was familiar with. There had been books, of course, written before, but quite infrequently. Maybe I was very close to that sort of life or close enough in order to make it palatable to somebody like that without necessarily brutalizing it or politicizing it in any way. I think there were always millions of working-class readers, a certain percentage, and if you go back to a period like the twenties and thirties or even before, they obviously read the classics, but stuff of a lesser quality than that would be sort of Bulldog Drummond and John Buchan, Edgar Wallace, Sexton Blake, and all that sort of stuff. So they weren't really catered for by something which I fondly hope is good writing and which also involves them.[4]

Sillitoe's comments here are trenchant, and find a lot of support in Hoggart's *The Uses of Literacy*.[5] Furthermore, Sillitoe recognizes the importance of the *mode* of publication as a reflection of the economic position of a working-class readership. Thus, he continues, "the hunger for paperbacks was manifest right from 1935 when the first ones began to appear."[6] What he does not note, however, is that by his own definition his first novel did not find its readership until two years after publication—and then only under special circumstances.

The paperback boom in England in the fifties and sixties was in large part driven by the voracious consumption of these books by the English working class. Working-class tastes not only helped to determine the genres of paperback fiction, but underlined the marginalization of the paperback as a mode of representation. It is interesting to note, for instance, that many of the books that appeared to offend establishment morality and the hardback predilections of the public library system were popularized by working-class paperback consumption. Such books as *Lolita, Catch 22,* and *Lady Chatterley's Lover* all received the nod from the working class while the "literati" were searching their critical vocabularies. Of course, we cannot say that working-class cultural consumption makes that culture working class, because we cannot assume that a class is only what it consumes. We can, however, identify those cultural products that are most readily available and circulated among a class as a measure of its *habitus,* to borrow again from Pierre Bourdieu.[7] One relevance of this to my study is that the working-class effects that Sillitoe hints at could not be realized in the hardback edition of *Saturday Night and Sunday Morning.* More importantly, the paperback of the novel was not only launched to utilize the paperback market as other working-class fiction of the period had done, but was specifically promoted as a tie-in to the film version of the book.

The contradictions of the cultural event, as an expressive formation of the cultural hegemony of ruling-class interests, are many, but one point in particular should be made here. Working-class fiction is guaranteed by the very ideological apparatuses that would exclude it. The processes of the "hard sell," the glamorization that Hoggart bemoans, actually facilitate the dissemination of positive images of the working class, as long as one remembers that these working-class effects are usually inside the package rather than in the packaging.

The Pan paperback edition of *Saturday Night and Sunday Morning* that appeared in 1960 features Albert Finney (who plays Arthur Seaton in the film) on the cover. His pose is confrontational, and his draped jacket completes the "angry" style.[8] Underneath the blurb reads, "makes *Room at the Top* look like a vicarage tea-party." The first print run was 150,000, but by the end of the year, after the film's successful London run, there were 600,000 copies in print and Pan gleefully described the sales as "absolutely phenomenal."[9] Sillitoe's work was not only available in every bookstore, but just about in every newsagent as well. The relationships between the writer's desired readership and the readership's desire is a complex one, but what I hope to have indicated here is that the mode of communication mediates whether any communication takes place, and that these relationships can be historically specified.

Sillitoe has recounted how it took him eight drafts and almost as many years to find the right voice for his expression, a voice rooted in his own experience. We should add that it took a further two years after publication before that voice was heard by those who shared a similar experience. But this raises another issue that I wish to address about working-class fiction and popular forms, an issue that I will approach through a theoretical consideration of the film version of *Saturday Night and Sunday Morning.* To analyze the transformation of the novel into the film is to further investigate the problem of representation of the working class, for it throws into relief some of the working-class effects of one form in relation to another. These distinctive elements will reappear in the theoretical exposition that ends this book.

Nineteen sixty was an important year for British working-class culture. It saw both the appearance of *Coronation Street* and the film version of *Saturday Night and Sunday Morning.*[10] Neither of these are the cultural products of the working class per se, nevertheless, they were/are "made" by the working class.

The number of British films that have ever made a genuine try at a story in a popular milieu, with working-class characters all through, can be counted on the fingers of one hand; and they have become rarer, not more frequent, since the war. . . . This virtual rejection of three-quarters of the population of this country represents more than a ridiculous impoverishment of the cinema. It is characteristic of a flight from contemporary reality by a whole, influential section of the community. And which is worse, by reason of their control of the cinema, they succeed in imposing their distorted view of the present on their massive and impressionable audience.[11]

Beyond any quibbles about fractions, reality, and the impressionable audience, Lindsay Anderson's viewpoint here marks an interesting moment in the history of representation of the English working class. Anderson's comments appeared in 1957 in *Declaration,* the undeclared manifesto of the Angry Young Men, and precisely prefigure the deluge of fiction films with working-class subjects in the five years that followed.[12] Anderson, of course, assumed a key role in projecting the proletariat, particularly in his association with the Wood-fall company, originally formed by Tony Richardson and John Osborne to make the film versions of Osborne's *Look Back in Anger* and *The Entertainer.* But it is clear that Richardson's plans for Woodfall were not quite the answer to Anderson's criticism: "It is absolutely vital to get into British films the same sort of impact and sense of life that what you can loosely call the Angry Young Man cult has had in the theatre and literary worlds."[13] Anderson is looking for a cinematic representation of the English working class; Richardson is suggesting a cinematic exploitation of an artistic cult. In event, the Woodfall films of the late fifties and early sixties are a curious amalgam of just these contradictory intentions.

The adaptation of Alan Sillitoe's *Saturday Night and Sunday Morning* was the most successful of Woodfall's proletarian films. I am going to follow two threads in examining this film. One interest concerns the conditions of possibility that determine the transformation of *Saturday Night and Sunday Morning* from novel to film, and I have already begun to hint at the historical dimensions of this cultural re-representation. Coterminously, I want to provide an analysis of how the film text represents the working class as subject and link this to the reception of the film as a means of understanding its ideological significance within what I have defined above as cultural event.

In the work of Bakhtin dialogism is a rich and complex theory on the nature of the word, particularly those that constitute the discourse of the novel. Certain aspects of this theory are useful for understanding the transformation of a novel into film. Dialogism recognizes that the word is a site of voicing; that is, that the word is the voice of a subject, but it may simultaneously voice the words or intentions of other subjects. Yet dialogism is not only useful for the analysis of the words of one particular form of discourse; it is also a way of exploring the interaction between different discourses, or texts. Julia Kristeva has investigated this possibility under the rubric of intertextuality but, as Robert Stam has explained,[14] it may be more accurate to use Genette's concept of hypertextuality as a specific instance of the dialogism of form. Hypertextuality refers to the dialogic relation of a "hypertext" to an anterior "hypotext": for instance, Joyce's transformation of the *Odyssey* into *Ulysses* or Gilbert Sorrentino's reworking of *Ulysses* in *Mulligan Stew*. Of course, the weakness of the term is that all texts are in some sense hypertextual, but nevertheless, as a word which describes the dialogic transformation and relation of one text to another it will be used in reference to the "cinematization" of *Saturday Night and Sunday Morning*.

If the Woodfall project was an attempt to make commercial films with working class themes, then *Saturday Night and Sunday Morning* must have seemed like a godsend. The book not only contained the angry aspirations that Woodfall had already popularized in Richardson's adaptation of *Look Back in Anger* (a success because, and in spite of, Richard Burton, the lead actor). It also could be read as a fictional working of the documentary techniques espoused by Richardson, Anderson, and Reisz in their "Free Cinema" phase, a desire to present people as they were, rather than an attempt to imagine the way others saw them.[15] I will return to the question of documentary technique later, but here it is important to note that Sillitoe himself had seen and approved of *We Are the Lambeth Boys* (1959), a film about a London youth club which Reisz had shot with the backing of the Ford Motor Company. Sillitoe's way of seeing, however, formed as it was from within the working class, was almost bound to be different from the gaze of the Woodfall group. As Roy Armes has noted, "For all their links with the late 1950s generation, Anderson, Reisz and Richardson in fact follow the pattern set by Grierson in the 1930s: the university-educated bourgeois making 'sympathetic' films about proletarian life, not analysing the ambiguities of their own privileged position."[16] Of course, a film may be more radical than the sympathetic intentions that make it, but Armes's point is well taken and underlines Richard Hoggart's major criticism of *We Are the Lambeth Boys*,—that there is a lack of focus on the "inner life" of its working-class subjects.[17] Sillitoe was naive to believe that Woodfall offered the possibility of simple translation into film of his novelistic skills and his political purview:

When I heard that *Saturday Night And Sunday Morning* was to be made into a film, and that I was going to be asked to write the script, I felt I was in for a tough exercise in resurrection. Nevertheless I agreed to it, mainly because I wanted a hand in the kind of film it was going to be. I didn't want Arthur Seaton . . . getting transmogrified into a young workman who turns out to be an honest-to-goodness British individualist—that is, one who triumphs in the end against and at the expense of a communist agitator or the trade unions. I didn't want him to become a tough stereotype with, after all, a heart of moral gold which has in it a love of the monarchy and all that old-fashioned muck.[18]

As scriptwriter, Sillitoe obviously made his intentions well known to Reisz, who took on the project with verve (Richardson had first choice for direction, but he opted for the role of producer). Indeed, it is clear from Reisz's initial feelings about the film that he wanted to avoid the kind of shortcomings outlined by Hoggart above. Arthur Seaton, Reisz observes, "is, if you like, one of the Lambeth Boys. An attempt is made to make a movie about the sentimental social education of *one specific* boy: thus the 'inner' things which the *Lambeth Boys* type of picture simply cannot apprehend . . . was attempted in *Saturday Night and Sunday Morning*. To put it more simply, and risking pretentiousness, the first work attempted a picture of a world, the second a portrait."[19] This desire to produce a portrait not only recalls the "honest to goodness" representation of individuality that had formerly been reserved for paintings of leading members of the ruling class, but also invocates a major *topos* of the feature film world that Reisz was trying to enter, the centrality of the lead character.

It would be wrong, however, to say that the aesthetic predilections of Sillitoe and Reisz were antithetical. Throughout his career, Sillitoe has consistently supported his statement in 1961 that he tries to see "every person as an individual and not as a class symbol."[20] Similarly, Reisz has said that Arthur was "by no means a standard-bearer for any ideas of mine. I never work with spokesmen. All my education, my teaching experience warned me of treating people as representatives of their world, rather than giving them the dignity of individuals; and I certainly disagree strongly with the idea that Arthur Seaton embodied my values, my outlook—I am a middle-class Jew from Central Europe."[21] It is not beyond the realm of possibility that Reisz's Jewish immigrant experience brought him closer to understanding Arthur and Sillitoe, as outsiders, than he is prepared to admit.

The individualist intentions of the writer and director, however they overlap, are overdetermined by the angry "cult" that Richardson identifies, and mediate the relations between hypotext and hypertext in distinct yet contradictory ways. For instance, what Anthony Aldgate calls the "contingencies of production" of the film compromise the "working-class effects" of the hypotext. On one level this meant toning down the language to get it past the British Board of Film Censors. Since I have argued for the centrality of language in working-class expression, the following excerpts from *BBFC* reports indicate the kind of institutional mediation that such expression undergoes:

I really don't think we can have "bogger," "Christ" or "sod." They ought to make do with the numerous "bleddys," "bloodies," "bleedings" and "bastards" which adorn the script. . . . I know that "bugger" is freely used in such places as the public bars of provincial pubs, but I doubt whether the average working man uses it much in his own home in front of his wife, and that ought to be more the standard for us to adopt, even in films obviously designed for the factory-worker section of society. (A great many young married men choose the films *they* want to see; their wives come with them and often don't enjoy the language, or the violence, at all.)

This script is peppered with "language" throughout . . . we would not accept "Christ," since many perfectly reasonable people take offence at this: we would particularly dislike "Christ Almighty" and "Christ-all-bleeding-mighty." Furthermore, we simply cannot accept the word "bogger." We have not yet accepted the use of the word "bugger" in films and the substitution of the letter "o" for the letter "u" makes no significant difference: on the soundtrack the word will certainly sound like "bugger." I appreciate that words of this kind are normal in the speech of the type of people that the film is about but I have always found, strange though it may seem, that these are the very people who most object to this kind of thing on the screen. I hope, therefore, that this script will be revised and these words omitted.[22]

The overt class prejudice that runs through these comments is guaranteed by the institutional context in which the judgments are offered. It is precisely this form of "semantic authority" that Bakhtin associates with the "monologic."[23] Here we do not have to mount some kind of defense of swear-words, for class intersects as much in these signs as any others; we are aware, however, that a specific use of "language" has been tailored by a social purview resistant to the "otherness" of Sillitoe's script. References to public bars, the notorious "average working man," and, since Britain was now supposedly classless, the factory-worker *section* of society clearly underline that it is as much who is using the language as the language itself that is the issue here. As for the word "bogger," Sillitoe uses the "o" as Aldgate points out, to indicate regional intonation, not as a sidestep to censorship (the *BBFC* prevailed, and "bogger" became the innocuous "beggar" in the film released). If, as I have argued above, the significant mark of working-class culture resides at the level of language, particularly in its reinscriptions of a prior oral tradition, then it would seem that the film version of *Saturday Night and Sunday Morning* is an important expression of such a culture. Much of the criticism on the film is, however, preoccupied with the "authenticity" of its dialogue as a projection of what the critic believes that world to be rather than undertaking an analysis of how the film *constructs* reality—a recognition that working-class effects are mediated prior to the critic's reflections on the real.[24]

Sillitoe's *Saturday Night and Sunday Morning* is a complex representation of working-class existence that depends on a fictive "inner" sociology to convey the lived social relations that power its narrative. The subjectivity of Arthur, for instance, can only be understood with reference to the intersubjective positions provided through the context-specific utterances of the book: as I have shown elsewhere, the subject positions of the narrative are established through the dialogic angles that Sillitoe's language attempts. Thus, the working-class effects of the book are not simply communicated by descriptions of working-class dress, eating and drinking rituals—the cultural capital of the working class is invoked by the materiality of the language of the book. This is not a concern with some vague notions of "authenticity," the dialogic relations of Sillitoe's book articulate nothing less than a mediation of the class consciousness of its interlocutors.

Reisz's *Saturday Night and Sunday Morning* is quite clearly, as hypertext, indebted to its literary precursor. But how does it interpret its anterior text? What are the determining factors of the film's re-representation? We have already noted that the film was the product, to a degree, of opportunism: to Woodfall it was the right film at the right time. On another level, we must say that Karel Reisz, as a filmmaker, is not too interested (and quite rightly) in a *faithful* rendering of Sillitoe's novel. The exigencies of form preclude an unreflexive mirroring of the novel in image and sound. This does not mean, however, that the hypotext cannot be worked in productive ways.

The film was shot in black and white, primarily for economic reasons; yet what this tends to do is emphasize the bleakness and drabness of the world revealed (it is an effect produced in many of the other films of the period, not the least of which is Richardson's version of "The Loneliness of the Long-Distance Runner").[25] Furthermore, the black and white underlines Arthur's "us and them" posturing within the narrative, his black-and-white world is an expression of his consciousness: it helps to define the enemy, like the foreman, Robboe (his white coat is the equivalent of the white robes of the Teuton, Ritter, in Eisenstein's *Alexander Nevsky,* and in this case stands out in sharp relief to the besmirched clothing of Arthur and the other workers at the factory).[26]

Both the novel and the film version of *Saturday Night and Sunday Morning* are realist texts; however, they are not the work of the same realism. The history of the production of the movie underlines some of the major differences, just as the film released confirms its relative cultural autonomy from the book that was its inspiration. Colin MacCabe's comments on the classic realist text are useful here:

> In the classical realist novel the narrative prose functions as a metalanguage that can state all the truths in the object language—those words held in inverted commas—and can also explain the relations of this object language to the real.[27]

The parallel in film is as follows:

> The narrative prose achieves its position of dominance because it is in the position of knowledge and this function of knowledge is taken up in the cinema by the narration of events. Through the knowledge we gain from the narrative we can split the discourses of the various characters from their situation and compare what is said in these discourses with what has been revealed to us through narration.[28]

MacCabe draws two main conclusions from this: (1) the classic realist text cannot deal with the real as contradictory; (2) in a reciprocal movement the classic realist text ensures the position of the subject in a relation of dominant specularity. In event, the different methods of realism in novel and film produce a similar closure in the classic realist text. But, as MacCabe notes, this does not extinguish the possibility of contradiction measured between the dominant discourse of the text and the dominant ideological discourse of the time. The will to struggle is not conveyed by the effect of contradiction, but by the *investigation* of it. In this sense, and perhaps this sense only, the realism of both the film and the novel hems in the progressive impulses of the subject.

The realist text is riven by the illusion that in representing the way things are, the reader/viewer sees things the way they are. Yet to represent is always to show *otherwise,* and to efface the production of otherness underlines the progressive potential of the realist text as highly problematic. Does this mean that the text which most self-consciously betrays its texual workings, its *repres-*entation is the one most privy to analyzing contradiction? Certainly there are many self-reflexive texts which share this progressive impulse. But I believe we must also entertain the possibility that realism can provide textual reflection in spite of itself—which is another way of saying that the novel and the film of *Saturday Night and Sunday Morning* are not examples that necessarily fit comfortably with classic realism, and can problematize its ruling conventions.

The film opens with a high-angle shot of a factory. It is the bicycle factory where Sillitoe worked as a young man. Reisz felt that there was little reason to construct a set that simulated this factory when they could shoot at the factory itself. Reisz wanted detail and realism and suggested that "the only way to get to know a place is to work there."[29] That Reisz was serious about this can be measured by his attempt to learn about the Nottinghamshire area before shooting Sillitoe's script. He even went so far as to make a documentary about a welfare center for miners in order to give him a feel for the locale. Reisz also got Albert Finney to learn to use the lathe that he operates in the film. This desire not to fake the details of Arthur's work in large part produces the cries about "authenticity" attached to the film. It also allowed Finney the chance to alter his approach to the material:

The reality of working the lathe, as an actor who'd just worked in the theatre for two years before these four, I found very exciting. When I was being photographed working at that lathe, then I could absolutely concentrate on what the character was supposed to do. There was no cheating involved you know. On stage it would have been made of cardboard and part of my job as an actor would have been convincing the audience that that cardboard lathe was an iron one.[30]

One further advantage in returning to the Raleigh factory was that Reisz invoked one of the striking characteristics of the novel: not just an attention to the working class, but to the working class in a working environment. We see Arthur in the working situation which to a large degree determines his world view in the story. It would be foolish, however, to see the factory location as an expression of the director's faithful recreation of this locale in the novel. Our vision of the factory is mediated at every level by the exigencies of form; that is, film conditions the reality of the factory differently from the reality effects endemic to the novel. It constitutes a re-representing of the narrative in ways that are appropriate to that form, and does so in a way that questions the subject position outlined in the MacCabe essay quoted above.

One example follows the opening shot I have mentioned. Sillitoe wrote three soliloquies for Arthur's character in the film, the third of which was not used as I will discuss later. The first soliloquy establishes the character of Arthur in the opening sequence. Arthur is at his lathe, finishing the last few components on his Friday shift. The soundtrack is full of the roar and bustle of the factory as the camera settles in to a medium shot of Arthur at work. The camera then cuts to several close-ups of Arthur's hands as they work the machinery. Arthur's voice is then heard over the noise of the factory as an interior monologue, delivered in a North Midland accent:

> Nine 'undred and fifty four. Nine 'undred and fifty bleddy five. Another few more and that's the lot for a Friday. Fourteen pounds three and tuppence for a thousand o' these a day. No wonder I've allus got a bad back—though I'll soon be done. I'll lark about a bit then, go and talk to the women—or the viewers. No use working every minute God sends. I could get through it in half the time if I worked like a bore, but they'd only slash me wages, so they can get stuck! Don't let the bastards grind you down. That's one thing you learn. Jack's one that ain't learnt. He wants to get on. Yes Mr. Robboe, no Mr. Robboe, I'll do it as soon as I can Mr. Robboe. And look where it got Robboe . . . a deadpan face and lots o' worry. Fred's alright. Knows 'ow to spend his money—like me, enjoys 'issen. That's more than them beggars know. They got ground down before the war and never got over it. I'd like to see anybody try to grind me down. That'd be the day. What I am out for is a good time. All the rest is propaganda.[31]

In ways that are specific to its context, Arthur's speech sets the narrative in motion in several ways. It identifies his relationship to his work; it establishes him as a major character within the story; it conveys an early sense of his rebelliousness, both with regard to Robboe and to the "climbers" like Jack (although we do not know at this stage that Arthur is having an affair with Jack's wife); and finally indicates that, unlike most worker stereotypes, Arthur is a thinking member of the productive process. What I have noted so far, however, are the verbal signifiers of literary analysis. This soliloquy comes into its own when it is considered as part of the filmic text, as a text that is much more than Sillitoe's screenplay.

As Arthur counts the components the camera cuts to a medium shot, which allows us to see Robboe, who enters the frame and gives Arthur his wage packet. Arthur then tells us about the wages, then the camera cuts to several point-of-view shots. Thus, we see Jack and Robboe as Arthur sees them and we are asked to identify with his position. Given the age and class of the majority of the English cinema-going public in the early sixties, we might say that at this moment Reisz has astutely "imaged" the viewer's reality, if not desire. Whether or not this was intentional need not concern us here for, as I have suggested earlier, working-class effects (either those of alienation, or identity) are not the product of artistic wish-fulfillment: they are historically specific. This can be underlined by the next shot when Arthur refers to Fred. From Sillitoe's comments on the script it is quite clear that of the two men in the frame, Fred is the black man. Yet in the published version of the script Fred is the white man working the machine, while "a black man loads it with raw material."[32] The point is, because of the spatial relations of the two figures to the camera Reisz has left it ambiguous who is who: the dominant specularity of which MacCabe speaks is not a unified one and on this occasion means that a potentially progressive statement is diffused.

The most powerful shot of the sequence is the last one. This is a low-angle shot of Arthur taken from a position seemingly within or slightly behind his lathe. This angle accentuates Arthur's sense of control over what he is doing just at the moment when his voice-over proclaims, "What I'm out for is a good time. All the rest is propaganda." This line is sharply punctuated by Arthur throwing down his oil rag, an action which both signals the end of his monologue and of work; but also the beginning of the main theme music of the film and the credit sequence.

In the scene above I would suggest that the cinematic practice employed goes beyond the formal constraints of the classic realist text defined by MacCabe; it points beyond the strategies of signifying containment that Barthes has characterized as "myth." The myth, or connotation, that other "working-class" films of this period prior to *Saturday Night and Sunday Morning* appealed to and seemed nourished by, was the notion of the "Angry Young Man." Burton's portrayal of Jimmy Porter in *Look Back in Anger* fosters the illusion that there are no brave causes left; Lawrence Harvey's character, Joe Lampton, rails against the British class system in *Room at the Top* while trampling over just about everybody, including his true love, in order to get ahead.[33] But if the film *Saturday Night and Sunday Morning* is in some sense produced by the same ideology that speaks through Porter's defeatism and Lampton's opportunism, there are also moments like the scene described above where that ideology is called into question, where it is internally distantiated in the Althusserian sense;

and not just by what Arthur says, but by the way his voice is presented. Thus, when Arthur contends that "All I am after is a good time. All the rest is propaganda," his polemical stance is externalized. But the way that this is shot provides a dialogic angle to this statement, a further *internal* polemic, to borrow from Bakhtin. The low camera angle gives an authority to what Arthur says, and shows him in control of the machine: now, presumably, we will see Arthur in spite of the propaganda.

For all Reisz's claims that his film sought to present an "inner world" that was not possible in the Free Cinema documentaries, critics have often remarked on the documentary, distanced style of *Saturday Night and Sunday Morning*. In defense of Reisz, George Gaston has attempted to show that camera distance in this film, although moderate, tends to underline close-up shots as moments of crisis; whereas long shots then serve to convey a continuous sense of deterministic environments. "This tension between moderate and extreme distancing is employed throughout the film in a rhythmic way, until distancing becomes one of Reisz's most expressive means of commenting on the situation before us."[34] Yet if the film is rhythmic, it is certainly more disjunctive than Gaston suggests. In effect, it supports the thesis that there are, after all, fundamental contradictions in the projection of working-class subjectivity in Reisz's realism.

It is not that camera distance, measured by the number of long shots employed, guarantees disinterestedness; the point is to assess whether the use of certain shots over others confirms a dominant specularity in contradiction with the subjective image that the film might offer. A pivotal scene in both the book and the film is where Arthur is finally cornered by the swaddies and made to answer for his "knocking around" with married women. The fight that ensues is shot in almost complete darkness. There is no dialogue or background music: all one hears are the occasional muffled sounds of body blows and crashing dustbins. All the action of this sequence takes place through a long shot which renders the perception image barely intelligible. In response to this we could say that Reisz is resisting the opportunity of glorifying the violent reproach to Arthur's dubious morality (indeed, most of the violence of the book is removed altogether, including the pub brawl and the overturning of a car). Such an argument would hold that the camera position takes Arthur's side in the fight because it does not flagrantly involve the viewer in Arthur's beating. If the earlier example of shot/reverse suture allowed positive audience identification with Arthur here the position of desire is radically altered. The dispassionate camera now appears to have abdicated the role of identification formation. Such a technique may well have positive implications, like the use of single tracking shots in Godard's *Weekend*,[35] but given the internal polemic suggested earlier one would have thought that this is precisely a moment of crisis deserving closer camera attention. The distance here allows the viewer the opportunity to avoid the consequences posed by identification with Arthur; those moments where the camera subverted the documentary view are now superceded by the semantic authority outside the viewer/character dialogue. It is as if Reisz himself has given up on the implications of his filmic style and resorted to the consoling morality of distance. What had been rendered so vividly in the book here becomes the film's major confusion. When, in the next scene, Arthur wonders "What am I? . . . God knows what I am," the viewer is in no position to share the import of this major existential question because positive identification has been sacrificed for a kind of voyeuristic calm.

Most critics of the film have remarked on its smooth pace, a nod perhaps to the principles laid out in Reisz's earlier book on film editing: "Constructing a smoothly flowing continuity has, indeed, become one of the modern editor's main preoccupations."[36] There can be no doubt that Reisz's principles of editing lend the film a continuity that cannot be found in the book; this is noticeable, for instance, where he uses the soundtrack to smooth transitions between one episode and the next. Yet there are moments, like the example given above, where the film is forced to face the logic of its own narrative structure. If part of the British "new wave" rationale was to attempt a cinematic realism that "constructs" working-class subjectivity, then it did so through more or less conventional cinematic narrativity, using suture as the mainstay of its identification technique. I have suggested that such identification processes, although usually frowned upon by radical theory, may have a progressive impulse when the subject in question is new to the screen. But when the mirror of identification is broken—and in the fight scene this is clearly the case—the processes of subject construction are called into question. One begins to wonder anew whether the classic realist text is bound by the strictures of its own informing world view to present the subject/object dialogue of working-class subjectivity (the working-class subject, as I have said before, as a process of intersubjectivity) as a monologic projection, as wish-fulfillment rather than critique.

This clash between narrative vision and "class effects" also manifests itself in the ending of the film. Here Reisz rejects both the ending of the book and Sillitoe's suggestions as screenwriter. The final scene shows Arthur and his new love Doreen on a hillside overlooking a new housing estate—a place where, presumably, they will set up home after their marriage vows. Arthur looks disconsolate and restless. Finally, he picks up a stone and throws it toward the new estate. Doreen here becomes the voice of reason: "You shouldn't throw things like that. The trouble with you is you never think." Arthur turns to her and replies, "I think enough, don't bother. It wain't be the last stone I'll throw either. Come on, let's get down." He tugs her by the arm and they saunter down the hill. The power of this scene might seem to rest in the continued sense of resilience in Arthur that it conveys. Thus, although marriage for Arthur is an act of conformity, he does not believe that it will fundamentally alter his antagonistic social attitudes. What is lacking, however, is a meaningful context for such attitudes. The utterance context within the narrative in this example suggests that Arthur might be running out of steam, and that throwing stones is just an empty act of resignation. It is interesting to note, therefore, that Sillitoe proposed an additional scene that, when combined with this one, would bolster the internal polemic established earlier in the story. In Sillitoe's screenplay the final scene finds Arthur back in the factory working at his lathe. Arthur's voice-over then ends the film with a third soliloquy:

> Jack's not all that bad. He's a good bloke in some ways. Lets the factory do as it likes with him though. They've bossed all the guts out of him. If he had any to begin with. There's thousands like him though: just love to be told what to do. I'll never get like that. Anybody opens their trap too much to me, gets it shut for 'em. Me, I was born fighting. Like I told Bert: you've got to fight in this world. But there's a bit of sweetness sometimes, and I know that much as well.[37]

Obviously it would not do to criticize Reisz for failing to adopt Sillitoe's intentions either in the book or the script. What one can say, however, is that in dropping this scene Reisz's film fails to live up to the premises with which it began. That is, it appears to falter according to its own intentions. What would the advantages have been in keeping this scene? First, it would have underlined that although Arthur has changed he has not given up; thus, there would be no ambiguity over the meaning of his stone-throwing. Second, the scene shows that Arthur has come to understand Jack, the cuckolded husband, if not respect him. Third, it shows Arthur working in the factory again.

The last point is important because it resists the idealism of the classic realist text that suggests that in love and marriage one somehow transcends the realities of work. In this respect, arguably the most effective scene of the working-class films of this period never reached the screen and for this film in particular, like the "missing" abortion scene, the absence of this sequence calls into question the political outlook of the project. Even with its significant box-office success and positive repercussions for the dissemination of Sillitoe's work, there is an overwhelming sense of a failure of nerve about this film. That the film openly challenged the mores and predilections of the Establishment cannot be denied, but its formal inconsistencies raise further issues about the modes of working-class cultural production in late capitalist society. These formal and theoretical issues are the subject of the next chapter.

# 6

# The Theory and Practice of Working-Class Fiction

From the time of my initial interest in Alan Sillitoe several years ago people have asked me "Whatever happened to Alan Sillitoe?" Well, he has not disappeared, but history moves in mysterious ways. As I write Alan Sillitoe has published a total of thirty-seven books, including seventeen novels, several volumes of short stories, six collections of poetry, five books for children, four plays, two travel books, and a collection of essays. The next book is no doubt at the press and will almost certainly be a novel. From the study I have presented so far, the mystery of Sillitoe's apparent disappearance is really no mystery at all. For the relations of cultural production which conjoined to produce the Angry Young Men can quite as effectively dismantle the stage on which their activities were played out. Sillitoe, I would argue, has produced significant fiction since the early sixties but has not enjoyed the same cultural context which made the earlier works reverberate with urgency. True, the quality of the work has been less than consistent yet this in itself insufficiently explains the critical neglect that Sillitoe has suffered. There are, however, sociopolitical reasons for Sillitoe's absent presence that go beyond an analysis of the trials and tribulations of an individual author's career. Indeed, the critique that I have provided so far should indicate some of the parameters of such an explanation. In this final chapter I want to draw on some of the lessons of my research, and to construct a dialectic of working-class fiction between practice that produces theory and theory that identifies and to some extent determines practice. If the first two chapters brushed history against the grain, and the next three attempted textual analysis in the same way, the following ruminations on form and subjectivity will at least be consistent to that degree, for here I intend to read postmodern theory otherwise. In any event, it may not help our comprehension of postmodernism but it may help to theorize our understanding of working-class fiction.

In writing about working-class fiction I have dealt with, in turn, a short story, a novel, and a film; a selection that, although it provides its own conscious displacement, is exclusionary. The cultural formation in which these forms were produced is obviously much more than this selection, and working-class cultural history is much more than this formation. Nevertheless, just as the focus on a single author allows some perspective on the limitations of individual production and reception, so too the accentuation of particular forms can have a strategic value in assessing "resistance" or "intervention." Procedural problems, of course, remain and these will be underlined in due course. For now I wish to address the class specificity of narrative form as a further examination of the sporadic appearances and disappearances of working-class fiction tracked through the first two chapters.

For many socialist critics the idea of a working-class novel is simply a contradiction in terms, but in my discussion of *Saturday Night and Sunday Morning* I tried to suggest that this contradictory nature may have productive consequences. There is simply no point in dismissing the novel outright since it has already provided a site for positive working-class expression. Nevertheless, a theory of working-class fiction that is overly dependent on the novel as form radically compromises the expressive collective subjectivity to which working-class culture often aspires.[1] This point certainly powers J. M. Bernstein's *The Philosophy of the Novel*. In reading Lukacs's *Theory of the Novel* through the developments of *History and Class Consciousness,* Bernstein attempts to show how the novel is a formal representation of the antimonies of Kant's philosophy; for instance, the novel organizes or constitutes a world in the same way that Kantian judgment constructs experience: for both, categorization is essential to the task of rendering experience meaningful and providing a rational narration of self. For Bernstein, in the dialectic of what is and what ought to be, the individualist narrativity of the novel becomes a form of remembrance of a collective storytelling, a substitution for a collective praxis the relations of bourgeois production must produce only to deny. Philosophically and politically the novel cannot create or interpellate a collective subjectivity because it is grounded on an interiorization of the social as self—an individual form-giving over and above the multiplicity of social subjects. Ultimately, the novel is condemned to describe an action for which it must always substitute, to *re*present a world that is always more than its form of apprehension.

Despite some of Bernstein's philosophical gymnastics, there is clearly much theoretical support for viewing the novel as the most form-bound prison-house of language.[2] Yet the "categorial contemplation" with which Bernstein locks the door between the novel and praxis suggests that any oppositional cultural practice that fights on the terrain of the novel is somehow always already doomed to defeat. In my study I have underlined the limitations of some cultural practices, overdetermined as they are by hegemonic relations (for instance, the staging aspect of the cultural event), but I have also noted time after time in the work of Sillitoe that the language of class does not passively fill the form in which it is produced. To this end, although Bernstein outlines the critical tendencies of the novel he takes these formal limitations as absolute. Of course the novel will never shake the foundations of capitalism for social transformation is always more than cultural practice; the obverse, however, is that without cultural contestation the *possibilities* of such transformation must seem the most abstract and rarefied of social options. In pursuing a philosophy of the novel Bernstein has overlooked the lessons of a philosophy of language.

One of the many values of the life work of Bakhtin is that he rigorously develops a philosophy of language to orient his formal analysis. As more than one critic has pointed out, however, the historicity he asserts for language becomes much less specific when he is dealing with the novel: the dialogic determinism of language riven as it is by class inflection does not seem to disrupt Bakhtin's idealist "novelization" of discourse. The rewriting of literary history in the image of the novel is ideologically suspect, let alone historically inaccurate. There seems no point in stressing the contextual workings of the utterance if its formal apotheosis is merely the novel. What we need is a theoretical apparatus that both avoids the disarming rhetoric of Bernstein's approach and the hypostatization of form in Bakhtin's discourse analysis.

The previous chapters point toward what shape such an approach might take. The story of working-class fiction is discontinuous for it always labors under various cultural relations of subordination. It is for this reason that we see in the nineteenth century the appearance of working-class subjects in the novel with relatively few examples where working-class subjects are in fact the agents of that production. This indeed is what makes Bruce Robbins's *The Servant's Hand* such an important work, for there he shows how the working class not only appear in what are predominantly bourgeois texts but also influence the mechanisms by which the narratives progress and conclude.[3] The content, therefore, disrupts the form and underlines the fragile narrative authority of the bourgeois text. Why working-class writers then come to contest and call into question the class specificity of the novel is not broached by Robbins, but the problem is clearly a significant "other" of the standard cultural histories of the period. First, such writing may be seen as part of a larger political struggle: the serialized novels of the Chartist press are the finest example of this form of approach. Second, writing of this sort can be seen as part of an ongoing struggle to appropriate what may seem inappropriate forms of expression and, rather than simply add a voice to the "democratic" dialogues of the novel, strike a note of discord beyond authorial intention because, as Williams notes, the working-class novel is not what a novel is supposed to be. Third, working-class appropriations of the novel from the nineteenth century into the twentieth are problematic not just in relation to broadly middle-class culture, but also more emphatically in relation to the storytelling traditions of the working class itself. This last point requires further examination.

Before the working class told stories through the novel they told stories; that is, oral narratives were and continue to be a significant part of working-class culture. Of course, no class has a monopoly on such a skill, but it should be stressed that what I have referred to as working-class fiction forms only a fraction of its narrative production: most working-class fiction only exists in the mouths and minds of its constituency. This is as true of the working class as it is of the "peasant" community of which John Berger so often writes:

> All villages tell stories. Stories of the past, even of the distant past. As I was walking in the mountains with another friend of seventy by the foot of a high cliff, he told me how a young girl had fallen to her death there, whilst hay-making on the alpage above. Was that before the war? I asked. In about 1800 (no misprint), he said. And stories of the very same day. Most of what happens during a day is recounted by somebody before the day ends. The stories are factual, based on observations or on an account given by somebody else. A combination of the sharpest observation of the daily recounting of the day's events and encounters, and of life-long mutual familiarities is what constitutes so-called village *gossip*. Sometimes there is a moral judgement implicit in the story, but this judgement—whether just or unjust—remains a detail: the story *as a whole* is told with some tolerance because it involves those with whom the storyteller and listener are going to go on living. . . . Very few stories are narrated either to idealize or condemn; rather they testify to the always slightly surprising range of the possible.[4]

Like Williams and Thompson, Berger shares a sense of the importance of community and experience in daily life. Here stories are integrated in the day-to-day existence of a community: they are crucial to the way a community defines itself, but they remain largely unwritten and unread. As Berger notes as he looks at the village storyteller, "I am writing on pages like these which he will not read."[5] Similarly, the railway stories that my grandfather told me have never been committed to paper, they only seemed to resonate in his mouth and the community in which we lived. Sid Chaplin, whose novel *The Day of the Sardine* was one of the few working-class stories not swept into the tide of the cultural event, was once asked whether it was the content of the oral tradition or the quality of the spoken word that influenced him most:

> Partly the content, yes, and partly the way it was told. They were marvellous storytellers. In fact, first of all I wanted to be a raconteur. I found out that I always missed the point of any story I was telling. Partly the reason that I'm a writer is that you can be more sure of getting the story right in writing it down, whereas a raconteur, you know, it just drops off his lips. It's the greatest art, oral storytelling, no doubt about it. But I haven't got the performer's ability; it's got to be born in you.[6]

What is interesting about Chaplin's comments is the way he contrasts oral and written skills in working-class storytelling. It is not a question of degree, so much as a different ordering of experience. For Chaplin, "getting it right" means writing the story correctly, not reproducing the thought processes, including lapses, of the raconteur. It is as if the working-class writer, even if she or he is not preparing for the realities of a middle-class audience as Spender suggests, must face the incommensurability of the novel with the way stories are told among working-class communities. Yet surely both representations of class knowledge share the same *episteme:* they are bound by objective class positions to "speak" in the margins of discourse. We would do well to heed the lessons of deconstruction regarding the bifurcation of speech and writing. Besides, as Benjamin has noted, "Experience which is passed on from mouth to mouth is the source from which all storytellers have drawn. And among those who have written down the tales, it is the great ones whose written version differs least from the speech of the many nameless storytellers."[7] Of course, his last point overlooks the ways in which writing mediates speech, a theme that I hope I conveyed in the analysis of the idiomatic insistence of Sillitoe's prose. Sillitoe himself has consistently wrestled with the problem of conveying oral stories through prose, which may be the reason that his short stories, his closest approximation to that tradition, have continued to draw some of his most approving criticism.[8] What this has tended to do is underline the difficulties of reproducing such skills in the novel. Sillitoe's most obvious and perhaps most flawed attempt was in *The Storyteller,* the tale of Ernest Cotgrave, a storyteller whose tales continually reveal the distance that Sillitoe has travelled from the oral tradition in which he was raised. David Craig describes the book as "forced and overwritten"[9] but does not address what is being forced—which I take to be an effort to build a narrative around a series of self-reflexive ruminations on how one tells a story. If there is a failure in imagination, it is that the "utterance contexts" of the oral delivery lack spontaneity in the written version. People do tell stories in pubs and launderettes, but why they do and the way that they do is not easily replicated in writing—in this sense, Chaplin's "getting it right" can turn out to be a hindrance. The only longer work apart from *Saturday Night and Sunday Morning* (which began as a series of short stories) where Sillitoe has given voice to the "many nameless storytellers" is the quirky *Raw Material,* a working-class autobiography masquerading as a discourse on "Truth" that is full of those little narratives of everyday existence that together describe the workings of a social group in terms which they themselves would use. Here Sillitoe describes a relative, "Eddie the Tramp":

> I last saw him on the top deck of a bus going from Radford into the middle of Nottingham. When we got off at Chapel Bar I gave him a copy of my first book of poems, called *Without Beer or Bread,* and he smiled at the title as he put it into his mackintosh pocket. I was about to go when, from an inside waistcoat, he brought an old fob-timepiece which he wanted me to have in exchange for the poems.
> "I can't take your watch."
> He smiled, the few teeth left in his mouth gone rotten. "It's only gold-plated zinc. It was with me at Gommecourt, and in Germany. Went all the time I was under fire. Would you believe it? Hasn't gone for years now."
> I looked at its clean Roman numerals on a round white face, a plain style I'd always liked,

its two hands stopped at four o'clock. "I often meant to get it going," he said, "but the pawnshop was closer than the watchmaker! They'd let me have a few bob on it but I'd allus redeem it before the time ran out."

"Let me give you some money for it," I offered, knowing this wouldn't insult him if he was broke, and that he'd be offended if I didn't take the watch. He tapped his pocket with my book in it: "Exchange is no robbery. Buy a chain for it, and get it ticking. I'd like to think the old thing's going to go again some time."[10]

I do not wish to ascribe some kind of essence to this micronarrative, the story of everyday life, because it is continually redefined both by the textual context of the utterance, and by the conditions through which that utterance is "read." What I do want to stress is that the heterogeneity of working-class experience, whether this example from the north Midlands or one from outside the focus on the English working class that I have taken, precludes analysis of working-class fiction on purely formal terms. There is no formal reason why a working-class novel should be privileged over a short story, film, play or the quasi-autobiography quoted above. To attempt such exegesis profers the danger of fetishizing form or merely producing in the parliament of the novel yet one more dutifully recognized genre—the working-class novel. What is important to address in theorizing working-class fiction is not form for form's sake, but the *struggles* over form. Sillitoe is an interesting case in point because we can track in his work an ongoing effort to give expression to a class-oriented world view and his fiction is open testimony to the power of the literary to "produce" class consciousness and indeed to be a product of consciousness. Particular form-giving at any one moment in history may be, in Bernstein's sense, politically stultifying but what is intriguing about working-class fiction is its incursions on the process of form-giving. It is small wonder therefore, that such analysis involves historicizing the discontinuous, for the struggles over form occur unevenly and with different historical parameters of development than with any single form.

Georg Lukacs's *The Historical Novel* is a well-crafted example of the single form approach, where he shows how the historical novel develops as a critique of bourgeois realism. An intraclass crisis in form is deemed symptomatic of the interclass confrontations that produce, for instance, the moment of 1848. Yet however we may laud the dialectical finesse of Lukacs's study it remains a top-down approach where cultural class war only seems to emerge in the novels of the bourgeoisie, particularly those associated with the nineteenth-century humanist tradition of bourgeois realism. As I have indicated earlier, this continues to have pertinent political value but one still awaits a full-length Marxist work on the *working-class* interrogation of form.[11]

Why such a critique is important is an issue implied in an essay by Philip Corrigan and Paul Willis on working-class cultural forms. There they stress proletarian forms as a "concretization" of discursive practices, a combinatory notion that counters the tendency to view working-class culture merely as a passive reflex to capitalist domination. It is interesting that some of their examples, particularly that of "factory discourse," are mediated in the dialogism at work in Sillitoe's fiction. For instance, they suggest that women workers can sometimes take on obviously *male* forms of speech (what they call "aggressive sexuality, explicit language, coarse exclusive humour")[12] to mimic and parody men in general, but also undermine the discursive authority of a male supervisor or foreman. In "The Good Women," Liza continually squares up against those who assume passivity on her part—like the shop steward who she calls "a fawce bogger" and the man who taunts her on street for being on strike: "You're a dirty Red" he bawls, and she retorts, "You'll be red if I smash my fist in your clock."[13] If it is true that shop floor culture blunts management control of the internal workings of industry, then we should not wonder that this social purview seeps through much of what I have been calling working-class fiction. The working-class effects, however, can hardly be called equivalent. To borrow again from Bakhtin's theory of sign, the utterances that may constitute resistance within the industrial complex are not merely reflected in fiction, they are refracted. Working-class fiction is not an approximation of working-class existence, but a cultural mediation of that reality. What this means is that whatever the correlation with factory discourse may be, the fictional representation of this world is not a challenge to what Corrigan and Willis refer to as the "structure in dominance" signified by the logic of capitalism at work in a factory; rather, the commitment to writing forces the utterance into a different context, a set of relations where it may challenge the *cultural* logic of capitalism. These two cultures, the discourses of everyday working-class life and the fictional representation of these discourses are relatively autonomous: Tressell's evocations of a strike do not have the same effect as the workers' strike where his book sold two hundred copies. Over such events critics have often rushed to identify the praxis of fiction (the crisis theory), yet as my work shows such an emphasis overlooks the historical urgency of the struggles *between* crises of which the problem of literary form is surely one. Just as the cultural spheres of capitalism are many and diffuse, so too are what Williams calls the "counter-hegemonic" cultural forms of the oppressed. If (especially in England) the concept of "literature" or the "literary" has attained and produced an ideological efficacy in the reproduction of capitalist social relations, then theorizing working-class fiction is an attempt to explain how certain ways of seeing contradict, displace, and deconstruct hegemonic ideologies. We should not prioritize these ways of seeing in terms of broader social change (in the contemporary crisis of Marxism, "motor of history" arguments, and the worker as transcendental subject are hardly unquestionable), but neither can we separate such work from political struggle altogether.

The historical, textual, and formal issues that I have raised so far are methods of addressing the changing problems posed by working-class fiction. To be sure, Sillitoe's work is not the quintessence of such fiction (however much theoretical desire would like to posit him as such), for it represents just one moment in a complex and discontinuous history; nevertheless, analysis of it can prove productive in mapping the possibilities of this form of counter-hegemonic production. As a final act of "reading" I want to consider the theory and practice of working-class fiction in relation to the key theoretical issues of our moment, a reflexive act that "reads" theory within poststructuralism and practice within postmodernism.

In the reading thus far it may seem that I have assumed an unreflective stance on the quality of realism in working-class fiction, yet such an assumption is not beyond criticism. Ken Worpole and Tony Davies, for instance, have both noted the problematic relation of realism to working-class expression.[14] Before the Second World War it was not uncommon to associate radical aesthetic experimentation with socialist politics—even with the moment of "high" modernism there is a concomitant leftist avant-garde whose work spans many national cultures.[15] Since the Cold War, however, these connections have not been critically persuasive and much working-class fiction has simply been read off against the prescriptive limitations of socialist realism—an association meant to recall, at least from a Right-wing perspective, the horrors of Stalinism. In Vaverka's "Marxist critique" of Sillitoe the tendency is to assume an essentialist model of realism in which this literary method itself becomes the guarantee of political perspicacity and therefore, unconsciously, offers itself up as proof that realism and working class are synonyms of the same sinister socialist realist aesthetic project. The contrast with my own study is that Sillitoe's realism is not taken to be some type of unmediated vision, however conscious Sillitoe may be of the literary method he employs. The reason for this is an historical compulsion: realism itself is overdetermined by cultural relations of production and dissemination; therefore, we can expect several versions of realism at any one moment in history. In the case of Chartist fiction, for instance, we can trace a realism caught up in the exigencies of the cultural conventions of penny fiction, while at the same time bourgeois realism takes a critical turn and assumes the "deep" form, as Williams calls it, that will come to be associated with many of the landmarks of nineteenth-century fiction. It is the latter that, as Catherine Belsey contends, articulates social relations through the construction of a hierarchy of discourses and appears to present history without a narrator while confirming omniscience as the guiding principle of subjectivity.[16] This, therefore, marks the emergence of the classic realist text that MacCabe is seen to bemoan in the previous chapter. Both Belsey and MacCabe would agree that the ideology of classic realism continues to dominate as a cultural mediation of the logic of capitalism whereby the commodity arrives without a producer; indeed, the commodity itself denies the process of labor that produced it. But just as capitalism is not a homogenous system of productive relations, so no one form of realism maintains a monolithic control over all others. Thus, the interrogative text of which Belsey writes may be antirealist in the classic sense, but nevertheless we should entertain the possibility that such a text may still be realist.[17] As we saw, the realist cinematic text of *Saturday Night and Sunday Morning* is constructed in an ambiguous relationship to models of classic realism and by no means simply confirms its central tenets. In what sense, however, can we ascribe this challenge, or internal distantiation (in the Machereyan sense) of the informing ideology of classic realism, to contemporary working-class fiction? Do the English working-class fictions of the late fifties and early sixties constitute the interrogative realist texts of their time?

I believe we can answer these questions in the affirmative although two initial provisos would be that Sillitoe is neither the embodiment of this challenge among working-class writers, nor are working-class novels the sole bearers of this critical stance. The point is to show that there are forms of cultural interrogation that are class-specific: a point that obviously argues against the disappearance of the working class subject or the permanent silence of that shadow-casting majority denigrated in Baudrillard's recent writing.[18]

One reason working-class fiction seems to appear and disappear in contemporary cultural debate is because the nature of capitalism itself has altered the way such work can be apprehended. From the discussion of the social situation of the postwar working class in chapter 2, we have some indication of the dynamics of these changes. Since the war there has been a commodification of indigenous working-class culture, a reappropriation of cultural expression and a "reprivatization of the recreational sphere of the working class."[19] This is also the moment of the cultural event, where working-class fiction can be staged as yet one more commodified episode in the "society of the spectacle," where working-class writers are interviewed, like other "stars," on the radio, and where *Coronation Street* is offered up as TV's ready barometer of working-class life. If anyone doubts the contradictions of late capitalism in the cultural sphere, the cultural event lays bare its ill-fated logic, for it works to deny class subjectivity at the very moment that it disseminates its most obvious recognition.

It is a fragmented subjectivity to be sure. I have tried to show through textual analysis how within this fragmentation itself we can discern the articulation of class effects at the level of language that together constitute a significant form of counter-hegemonic cultural expression. The temptation is, of course, to hold up characters like Liza Atkin and Arthur Seaton as some kind of working-class heroes, as if their stories offer the security of their respective subject positions in society as a whole. Bakhtinian discourse analysis is useful here because the principles of dialogism stress the socially interactive possibilities of the utterance without making a fetish of individual semantic authority (the main drawback of individualistic subjectivism). It is for this reason that I have stressed the intersubjective quality of discourse, a hypothesis that proves particularly fruitful in analyzing class-specific writing. In this sense the important feature of working-class fiction is not that individual characters are the embodiment of the working class; rather, the working class is intimated through a compendium of interchanges between addressers and addressees within and without the story. Thus, the "working classness" of fiction is not measured by the multiplicity of subject positions that discourse enunciates, but the intersubjective exchanges of dialogic discourse. In short, working-class fiction is not just a question of who is speaking, but also of who is the prospective listener and under what circumstances their interaction takes place. It is only in the linguistic space between subjects that we can speak in terms of a working-class stylistic in fiction: the dialogic angling of the utterance is the medium of class ideology, a social purview that is always more than individual characteristics, more than the individual subject. If Bakhtin is right to claim sign as an arena of class struggle there seems no better proof than in the intersubjective exchanges of working-class fiction.

In his essay "Post-modernism, or the Cultural Logic of Late Capitalism," Frederic Jameson discusses a wide range of elements associated with the postmodern break or *coupure* from the late fifties on. The working-class fiction I have discussed does not fit neatly into Jameson's conception, nor do I want to make it so. Sillitoe's work shares none of the aesthetic populism Jameson describes in relation to architecture or the critical historicism of E. L. Doctorow. Although the same social relations appear to obtain, there seems no obvious sense in ascribing the texts I discuss to the postmodern aesthetic:

> What has happened is that aesthetic production today has become integrated into commodity production generally: the frantic economic urgency of producing fresh waves of ever more novel-seeming goods (from clothing to airplanes), at ever greater rates of turnover, now assigns an increasingly essential structural function and position to aesthetic innovation and experimentation.[20]

There is little conscious innovation or experimentation in the fiction dealt with herein. What I have argued however, is that the cultural relations of the period take up working-class expression as an innovative commodity and market it as such. For a while at least, it became fashionable to be working class—for instance, some of the London culturati even affected Cockney accents. More importantly, the marketing of the working class was directed at the working class as consumers, an uneven process to be sure, and one not fully successful until the advent of the Beatles. Thus, although the postmodern as cultural dominant does not drive the working-class fiction discussed, it certainly effects its dissemination. Indeed, what it confirms are the disarming propensities of postmodern cultural relations, for the "Us and Them" polemics of Sillitoe are quickly packaged and reabsorbed into the general system of cultural exchange. What is curious (or maybe not so curious) is that although work like Sillitoe's is clearly out of step with the postmodern aesthetic and ideologically antibourgeois, it quickly became drawn into the center of cultural debate. Since I have argued that such work constitutes a cultural intervention this last point requires further consideration.

Two distinctions should be made. The first is that although postmodern cultural *relations* produce the cultural event in which working-class fiction is interpellated, the late capitalist "will to commodify" does not somehow naturally seek postmodern art. In this light the disjunction offered by Sillitoe's work is therefore hardly surprising. The second distinction concerns postmodernism in relation to cultural formations. If we accept Jameson's proposition that postmodernism is not a style but a cultural dominant, this does not mean that its major characteristics permeate every level of cultural production and exchange; they merely *condition* the possibilities of such activity. The cultural event as I have described it is precisely the expression of postmodern conditioning. In staging working-class subjectivities however, cultural relations conjoin to produce a moment where the logic of cultural hegemony itself is called into question and its principles of exclusivity break down. This is why it is important to attempt to understand working-class fiction in relation to postmodernism, for to believe that working-class writing (at least in the West) can somehow exist outside the dominant cultural relations of our time is simply to confine such fiction from the most pressing arenas of cultural struggle.

One conclusion from what has been said so far may be that the cultural event itself proves that working-class fiction is no longer considered the oppositional threat that it clearly constituted in the thirties. Our historical analysis shows that although the cultural relations of working-class fiction have altered, it continues to be constituted as subaltern or marginal writing. As Raymond Williams explains, working-class writing seems "residual" because it appears dependent on the cultural residue represented by the nineteenth-century realist novel.

A residual cultural element is usually at some distance from the effective dominant culture, but some part of it, some version of it—and especially if the residue is from some major area of the past—will in most cases have had to be incorporated if the effective dominant culture is to make sense in these areas. Moreover, at certain points the dominant culture cannot allow too much residual experience and practice outside itself, at least without risk. It is in the incorporation of the actively residual—by reinterpretation, dilution, projection, discriminating inclusion and exclusion—that the work of the selective tradition is especially evident. . . . It is in some alternative or even oppositional versions of what literature is (has been) and what literary experience (and in one common derivation, other significant experience) is and must be, that, against the pressures of incorporation, actively residual meanings and values are sustained.[21]

This helps to explain why postmodernism, as cultural dominant, attempts to address and "incorporate" forms of literature that, as actively residual, challenge the central tenets of its dominance. By this I do not mean to raise the banner of older forms of class war (i.e., that these cultural disjunctions come to polarize around more or less homogenous versions of bourgeois versus proletarian), but rather to suggest that these examples of cultural struggle point to the importance of class analysis in theoretical debate. The war over words traced through the work of Alan Sillitoe underlines that the dialogism of the oppressed is not merely a quirk of history, but an active component of contemporary struggle.

Is working-class fiction confined to the residual, condemned to draw on the heroic possibilities of an age that is gone? Just as the postwar English working class has been reconstructed, the forms of its cultural expression are also subject to change. Why then the continued obsession with realist fiction? On the one hand there is more than enough evidence, as Ken Worpole has shown, that working-class fiction is much more than just realist;[22] on the other, realism itself has not appeared in my work as an unproblematic set of textual conventions. As Tony Davies notes:

> [R]ealism, in all its multiple incarnations, is not really a literary form or genre on [sic] movement or tradition at all but a contested space, the scene of an unfinished argument. Defined in this way, realism is likely to appear, from a literary-critical point of view, little more than an attitude, a pious hope without substance or consistency. But the business of working-class writing never did look, from that point of view, particularly important or even real. Leavis's sneer about "the duty of the writer to identify himself with the working class," and his contemptuous assignation of such self-evident *betises* to the "Marxizing" thirties, are typical enough, and point to a general abandonment of the issues, as well as to a dyspeptic and complacent parochialism that is specially English. In the post-war years, when not only working-class writing but the working class itself has been widely reported to be little more than a sentimental anachronism, literary criticism has gone about its business, "placing" here and "evaluating" there, very busily and self-importantly indeed. Only recently has it started to develop headaches, and to sleep badly at nights. But it is not thought that this has anything to do with the unfinished business of realism, or with bad dreams about the working class.[23]

I do not believe that realism is quite the open field of battle that Davies suggests: institutionalized forms of realism require specific analysis of their particular codes and practices. Nevertheless, the notion of struggle implied above is pertinent to much of the "angry" production discussed in this book. Similarly, the nightmares of literature departments are not solely due to the working class, although their fiction—alongside that of women and so-called "minorities"—together constitute a monstrous id that is not easily repressed. As part of a broader cultural debate, Davies's points are well taken and underline that even amongst the discursive heterogeneity of postmodernism there is specific unfinished business to be addressed. Yet not all of the business of working-class fiction need concern itself with the problem of realism.

In the work of Williams, residual and dominant are but two of the cultural processes discussed; the third is the emergent, and provides the most provocative analogy to the productive possibilities of working-class fiction:

> A new class is always a source of emergent cultural practice, but while it is still, as a class, relatively subordinate, this is always likely to be uneven and is certain to be incomplete. For new practice is not, of course, an isolated process. To the degree that it emerges, and especially to the degree that it is oppositional rather than alternative, the process of attempted incorporation significantly begins. . . . The process of emergence, in such conditions, is then a constantly repeated, an always renewable, move beyond a phase of practical incorporation: usually made much more difficult by the fact that much incorporation looks like recognition, acknowledgement, and thus a form of *acceptance*.[24]

This, I would suggest, posits the central challenge of working-class fiction. Working-class writers may well have to appropriate residual forms to express themselves for they should express themselves "by any means necessary." But alongside such efforts the specific social situation of the class will impel cultural expression that resists "practical incorporation." The cultural event of the late fifties and early sixties seems bound up in complex relations of incorporation and resistance. Some of the activities of the writers involved clearly lent themselves to incorporation, particularly with regard to the "myth" of the Angry Young Man. Resistance took many forms, but what I have stressed is the opposition generated by the language styles of the fiction; such class orientations are not easily effaced by generalizations about anger and despondency. What is difficult to measure, although the concept of dialogism has proved helpful, are the precise elements of oppositional discourse that together constitute a counter-hegemonic cultural formation. According to Williams, this may be understood by consideration of what is "active and pressing"—what are called the "conditions of pre-emergence," or "structures of feeling."[25] In part my study has taken this up by stressing the role of experience in the production of ways of seeing. There are drawbacks to Williams's view and my own, in that overstressing the "lived" and "felt" can all too easily plunge one back into a quagmire of subjectivism deep enough to drown most theoretical positions. My own defense, as you will have noticed, has taken the form of several decentering strategies: when I could have argued for the homogeneity of class expression I have opted for difference; when I could have underlined semantic authority I have stressed the overdeterminations of language; when I could have constructed some form of tradition I have argued for discontinuities; and when conventional accounts of subjectivity were available I have chosen intersubjectivity. These, I believe, are the means to theorize experience because they address its current fragmentary nature. That the production of working-class fiction therefore does not equal conventional accounts of class underlines that class-specific fiction itself is not a guarantee of class praxis. Nevertheless, in emphasizing the activity of working-class writers as *producers* we can open the way to an understanding of such fiction as cultural agency, an articulation of "structure of feeling in solution,"[26] which may, or may not, be a guarantee of material practice beyond the fragments. In this the dialogism of the oppressed indeed confirms language as a site of class struggle and working-class fiction itself as a discourse of resistance and opposition. It also suggests that both the theory and practice of working-class fiction are counter-hegemonic spheres of interest: they fight different battles on different terrains yet both are concerned with elements of social change and both are cognizant, like Liza Atkin, that sometimes words may not be enough. But neither indeed is silence.

In this study I have not pretended to speak for Sillitoe, nor indeed do I assume that in my work he can merely speak for himself—there are ways, in fact, that we are both spoken. This is as true for us as it is for his characters whose private pronouncements "read" more like collective desire. This realization is nowhere more prominent than in Smith, the Borstal boy of "The Loneliness of the Long Distance Runner." Again, like Liza and Arthur, Smith is not typical of the working class, yet voices a structure of feeling that is specific to it. Although his battle is often intensely private, especially with the warden of the institution, the staging of this political position is overdetermined by a collective subjectivity which Smith speaks as "us." In any event, the triumph of his own battle, in deliberately losing the cross-country race, is a deferred victory in the individual and the collective sense, for Smith knows, as we should, that coming to political consciousness is not in itself the act of overcoming "them," but a prelude to such an act. This realization defines Smith's loneliness, and for my purposes, helps to explain the practice of writing working-class fiction *in relation* to working-class praxis. Perhaps the political importance of this final quote from Smith is then as yet another beginning, a step to reading and writing the working class that underlines that historical analysis is not just a recuperative exercise, but a means of addressing current contingencies.

No, I won't get them that cup, even though the stupid tash-twitching bastard has all his hopes in me. Because what does his barmy hope mean? I ask myself. Trot-trot-trot, slap-slap-slap, over the stream and into the wood where it's almost dark and frosty-dew twigs sting my legs. It don't mean a bloody thing to me, only to him, and it means as much to him as it would mean to me if I picked up the racing paper and put my bet on a hoss I didn't know, had never seen, and didn't care a sod if I ever did see. That's what it means to him. And I'll lose that race, because I'm not a race horse at all, and I'll let him know it when I'm about to get out—if I don't sling my hook even before the race. By Christ I will. I'm a human being and I've got thoughts and secrets and bloody life inside me that he doesn't know is there, and he'll never know what's there because he's stupid. I suppose you'll laugh at this, me saying the governor's a stupid bastard when I know hardly how to write and he can read and write and add-up like a professor. But what I say is true right enough. He's stupid, and I'm not, because I can see further into the likes of him than he can see into the likes of me. Admitted, we're both cunning, but I'm more cunning and I'll win in the end even if I die in gaol at eighty-two, because I'll have more fun and fire out my life than he'll ever get out of his. He's read a thousand books I suppose, and for all I know he might even have written a few, but I know for a dead cert, as sure as I'm sitting here, that what I'm scribbling down is worth a million to what he could ever scribble down. I don't care what anybody says, but that's the truth and can't be denied. I know when he talks to me and I look into his army mug that I'm alive and he's dead. He's as dead as a doornail. If he ran ten yards he'd drop dead. If he got ten yards into what goes on in my guts he'd drop dead as well—with surprise. At the moment it's dead blokes like him as have the whip-hand over blokes like me, and I'm almost dead sure it'll always be like that, but even so, by Christ, I'd rather be like I am—always on the run and breaking into shops for a packet of fags and a jar of jam—than have the whip-hand over somebody else and be dead from the toenails up. Maybe as soon as you get the whip-hand over somebody you do go dead. By God, to say that last sentence has needed a few hundred miles of long-distance running.[27]

# Notes

## Introduction

1. Alan Sillitoe, *The Loneliness of the Long Distance Runner* (London: W. H. Allen, 1959), p. 48. You will note Smith's significant absence from most of the following text, although I do seem to have given him the "last" word.

2. William Empson, *Some Versions of Pastoral* (New York: Books For Libraries Press, 1972). This is a reprint of the 1938 edition.

3. D. M. Roskies, "Alan Sillitoe's Anti-Pastoral," *Journal of Narrative Technique* 10 (1980): 170–85.

4. Empson, p. 19.

5. One exception is the work of Michael Denning. See his *Mechanic Accents* (London: Verso, 1987).

## Chapter 1

1. E. P. Thompson, *The Making of the English Working Class* (New York: Vintage, 1966), p. 9.

2. Here is not the place to recount Thompson's orrery of reproach which can be consulted in Thompson's *The Poverty of Theory and Other Essays* (New York: Monthly Review Press, 1978), pp. 1–210. To understand the bitterness of Thompson's attack, one should perhaps consult his preface to that volume. Although appreciating the seriousness of Thompson's historiography, his attempt to embarrass Althusserianism has its own embarrassing moments, witness the flippancy of the "structuralist" diagrams that adorn his text. For a pertinent forum that places Thompson's argument within an English context see Terry Eagleton et al., "E. P. Thompson's *Poverty of Theory:* A Symposium," *Literature and History* 5 (1979): 139–64. Unlike Thompson, I do not intend to throw the baby out with the bath water.

3. Thompson, *Poverty,* pp. 298–99.

4. In addition to the forum mentioned above Perry Anderson's discussion of the debate is particularly instructive. See Perry Anderson, *Arguments within English Marxism* (London: Verso, 1980), pp. 1–58.

5. Anderson, pp. 16–18.

6. See, for instance, the last chapter of Karl Marx, *Capital* (volume 3).

7. This, of course, explains why the importation of Althusser's reading of Marx, in which ideology always already interpellates subjects, proved so volatile in an English intellectual climate where subjects, in Thompson's case, still made history. My interpretation will suggest that cultural production is riven by ideological constraints (an acceptance, to a degree, of Althusserian interpellation) but that cultural agents may intervene and disrupt the reproduction of the relations of production at the level of culture. Their agency does not constitute a social transformation in itself, but neither does it make working-class cultural producers passive receptacles of bourgeois culture.

8. Walter Benjamin, *Illuminations,* ed. Hannah Arendt, trans. Harry Zohn (New York: Schocken, 1969), p. 83. The storytelling of the future, one would hope, will no longer be bound by the social determinations of class.

9. Gustav Klaus, *The Literature of Labour* (New York: St. Martin's Press, 1985), p. ix.

10. Pierre Zima, *Manuel de Sociocritique* (Paris: Picard, 1985), p. 22. Zima uses this term in discussing the work of Gramsci. Later I will consider the subaltern through Gayatri Spivak's work on the subject. See chapter 4.

11. The point here is not to ascribe a monopoly of class effects to writers born within the working class but to underline the importance of specific social relations in the formation of class purview.

12. There is much confusion over the status and availability of Ashraf's work in English. The important book is *Englische Arbeitliteratur vom 18. Jarhundert bis zum Ersten Weltkrieg.* My attempts to obtain a copy were unsuccessful, although Klaus insists that an English stencilled version of the book is circulated in the German Democratic Republic. The Germans continue to provide the most detailed research on English working-class writing, although the Centre for Contemporary Cultural Studies in Birmingham provides at least the potential for English interest. My bibliography includes works from both countries.

13. See Klaus, p. 8.

14. Karl Marx and Friedrich Engels, *The German Ideology* (London: Lawrence and Wishart, 1963), pp. 40–41.

15. I will deal with this in more detail later. The relevant text is Gareth Stedman Jones, *Languages of Class* (Cambridge: Cambridge University Press, 1983).

16. P. J. Keating, *The Working Classes in Victorian Fiction* (London: Allen and Unwin, 1971), p. 124.

17. Keating, p. 3.

18. Martha Vicinus, *The Industrial Muse* (London: Croom Helm, 1974), pp. 60–93; "'To Live Free or Die': The Rhetoric and Style of Chartist Speeches, 1838–9," *Style* 10 (1976): 481–503; and "Chartist Fiction and the Development of a Class-Based Literature," in Gustav Klaus, ed., *The Socialist Novel in Britain* (Brighton: Harvester Press, 1982), pp. 7–25.

19. Vicinus, "Chartist Fiction," p. 7.

20. Ibid., p. 23.

21. Quoted in Klaus, *Literature,* p. 50. Both the arguments of Klaus and Vicinus underline the claim that Chartist fiction was inextricably tied to other modes of political intervention in the movement. My point is that the development of cultural and political practices is far from even,

and that Chartist fiction should not be taken as the norm by which all subsequent working-class writing should be measured.

22. The idea of utterance context is a crude way to integrate writing and speech in discourse theory. Although Bakhtin was rarely consistent or particularly explanatory in developing this concept, I explore its possibilities in chapters 3, 4, and 5.

23. Quoted in Klaus, *Literature*, p. 49.

24. I am quoting from the essay translated from *Le Degré Zéro de l'écriture* (Paris: Editions du Seuil, 1953) for *Yale French Studies*, and subsequently published in Jacques Ehrmann, ed., *Literature and Revolution* (Boston: Beacon Press, 1967), p. 79. This translation differs considerably from that published by Hill and Wang.

25. See Vicinus, "Chartist Fiction," pp. 19–21; Klaus, *Literature*, pp. 54–56; and Jack Mitchell, "Aesthetic Problems of the Development of the Proletarian-Revolutionary Novel in Nineteenth-Century Britain," in David Craig, ed., *Marxists on Literature* (London: Penguin, 1975), pp. 255–59. Mitchell claims that Wheeler's *Sunshine and Shadow* is the forerunner of the "modern proletarian novel" because he relates an individual political development of character to the development of an organized mass movement. This, I would suggest, marks the chief difference between proletarian and working-class fiction, for the latter encompasses class-specific writing that may appear in the *absence* of an organized mass movement. As we will see, this difference is crucial to an understanding of the period I analyze in the next chapter.

26. Raymond Williams, *Writing in Society* (London: Verso, 1983), p. 153. Williams's conception of the "deep form" is an attempt to explain how the major industrial novelists manage the ideological contradictions of their class position in relation to the proletariat. In identifying their repressions and resolutions Williams comes about as close as we could expect to the Althusserian position on ideology and culture (the imaginary resolution of real contradictions). He wriggles out of it by suggesting that there are different degress of ideological reconciliation, but the similarity remains.

27. Williams, p. 163. The notion of deep form will be discussed in relation to Williams's idea of "emergent" cultural forms later in this chapter.

28. Williams, p. 165.

29. George Orwell, "Charles Dickens," *Inside the Whale* (London: 1940), p. 11. Bruce Robbins's work shows how middle-class Victorian writers negotiate the absence of the working class in their texts by granting them an effective presence in the form of servants who, at some points, even become the agents who function to develop individual narratives. See Bruce Robbins, *The Servant's Hand* (New York: Columbia University Press, 1986).

30. Stedman-Jones, pp. 21–22. Stedman-Jones has sparked a lively debate in English Marxist historicism that draws much of its sustenance from the older Thompson/Althusser disputes. Stedman-Jones's particular penchant for "class" as a discursive category has produced a lengthy response from John Foster, whose historiography is the subject of Stedman-Jones's second chapter. See John Foster, "The Declassing of Language," *New Left Review* 151 (1985): 29–45.

31. J. M. Rignall, "Between Chartism and the 1880s: J. W. Overton and E. Lynn Linton," in Gustav Klaus, ed., *The Socialist Novel in Britain* (Brighton: Harvester Press, 1982), p. 26.

32. Raymond Williams, "Working Class, Proletarian, Socialist: Problems in Some Welsh Novels," in Klaus, ed., p. 114. Both Williams and Klaus have remarked upon the lack of working class novels in Britain in the nineteenth century, but where Klaus provides more empirical documen-

tation, Williams has a deeper theoretical comprehension, particularly regarding cultural formations.

33. The concepts of habitus and cultural capital derive from the work of Pierre Bourdieu. Briefly, class habitus describes the shared code developed within class that results, to a degree, from the homogeneity of the conditions of existence of that class. Habitus is the matrix of perceptions, appreciations, and actions that together constitute a world view or social purview in Bakhtin's terms. See in particular Pierre Bourdieu, *Outline of a Theory of Practice,* trans. Richard Nice (New York: Columbia University Press, 1977), pp. 78–87. Cultural capital describes class and subclass differentiations constructed through hierarchies of taste. Since taste is a top-down distinction, the working class can be precisely defined by their relative lack of cultural capital—those distinctions held to be the hegemonic tastes of the bourgeoisie. See Pierre Bourdieu, *Distinction,* trans. Richard Nice (Cambridge: Harvard University Press, 1984).

34. See, for instance, John Lucas, ed., *The 1930s: A Challenge to Orthodoxy* (Brighton: Harvester Press, 1978); and John Clark et al., eds., *Culture and Crisis in Britain in the Thirties* (London: Lawrence and Wishart, 1979).

35. Ramon Lopez Ortega, "The Language of the Working Class Novel of the 1930s," in Klaus, ed., p. 122.

36. Lopez Ortega, p. 124.

37. See in particular, Basil Bernstein, *Class Codes and Control,* Vol. 1 (London: Routledge and Kegan Paul, 1971). In general I have avoided rooting working-class language in Bernstein's concept, opting for the less absolute discourse theory of dialogism to be found in Bakhtin's work. This will be discussed in due course.

38. The parameters of such an investigation are at least suggested in Terry Eagleton, *Criticism and Ideology* (London: Verso, 1976), pp. 157–61.

39. Peter Miles, "The Painter's Bible and the British Workman: Robert Tressell's Literary Activism," in Jeremy Hawthorn, ed., *The British Working Class Novel in the Twentieth Century* (London: Edward Arnold, 1984), p. 4.

## Chapter 2

1. Alan Sinfield, *Society and Literature, 1945–1970* (London: Methuen, 1983), p. 5. There is a growing body of work in this area, typified to some degree in the writings of the Birmingham Centre for Contemporary Cultural Studies. For an overview see Peter Widdowson, ed., *Re-Reading English* (London: Methuen, 1982). For two studies that discuss the mediation of criticism within an institutional problematic see, Peter Uwe Hohendahl, *The Institution of Criticism* (Ithaca: Cornell University Press, 1982); and Francis Mulhern, *The Moment of 'Scrutiny,'* (London: Verso, 1979).

2. Here I invoke Sheila Rowbotham's feminist analysis, *Hidden from History* (London: Pluto, 1973). It seems to me that it is imperative that socialists learn the lessons of feminist historiography in order to attempt a rediscovery of the working classes in cultural history. Two works that read very much like this are Ken Worpole, *Dockers and Detectives* (London: Verso, 1983); and Gustav Klaus, *The Literature of Labour* (New York: St.Martin's Press, 1985).

3. See Daniel Bell, *The End of Ideology* (New York: Harper and Row, 1962). Recently the trope of the failure of grand narratives has surfaced again in the form of French poststructuralism,

see Jean-Francois Lyotard, *The Postmodern Condition* (Minneapolis: University of Minnesota Press, 1984). The prospects of "immaterialism" are highly ambiguous, however, as I discuss in my final chapter.

4. The standard texts are *Capital, Theories of Surplus Value,* and the work on political economy, *Grundrisse.* For an application of Marxian principles to global capitalism see Ernest Mandel, *Late Capitalism* (London: Verso, 1978). For a discussion of the problems of Marxian analysis in our current historical moment see Stanley Aronowitz, *The Crisis in Historical Materialism* (New York: Praeger, 1981).

5. This is discussed by Richard Hoggart, *The Uses of Literacy* (London: Chatto and Windus, 1957), particularly the conclusion. For a more recent critique see Trevor Blackwell and Jeremy Seabrook, *A World Still to Win* (London: Faber, 1985).

6. See above Blackwell and Seabrook. Also K. Roberts, *The Working Class* (London: Longman, 1978), and John Westergaard and Henrietta Resler, *Class in a Capitalist Society* (London: Pelican, 1976). Both these are general survey books.

7. See Arthur Marwick, *British Society since 1945* (London: Pelican, 1982), pp. 114–85.

8. Doris Lessing, *A Small Personal Voice* (New York: Vintage, 1975), p. 20.

9. See Anderson, *Arguments* et al. in chapter 1.

10. Richard Hoggart, pp. 171–223.

11. See the introduction to Denys Thompson, ed., *Discrimination and Popular Culture* (London: Pelican, 1964). Note, I am not contending that their alternatives to the dangers posed by massification are the same, but that their appeals to discrimination underestimate the productive potential of the consumer within mass culture. It is more than a matter of choice as the punk *bricoleurs* have already proved.

12. Of course, Williams did have the Scrutiny group as many critics have pointed out. For the possible drawbacks of that influence see Terry Eagleton, *Criticism and Ideology* (London: Verso, 1976), pp. 11–43. Sillitoe too was not unaware of certain literary influences, but most of them fell outside the working class itself. One is tempted to draw comparisons with Lawrence, and indeed Sillitoe believes Lawrence to be a "great, great novelist." What I am suggesting, however, is that much of the influence was alien to Sillitoe's experience. As Sillitoe recounts, "So my early novels, unpublished, thank God, were pastiches of Dostoevski, Lawrence, Huxley, Forster—you name it, they obviously rolled in, and then, fortunately again, they rolled out." John Halperin, "Interview with Alan Sillitoe," *Modern Fiction Studies* 25 (1979): 179.

13. Raymond Williams, *Culture and Society* (London: Penguin, 1961), p. 268.

14. Halperin, p. 178.

15. Williams, *Culture and Society,* pp. 11–12.

16. Richard Johnson, "Three Problematics: Elements of a Theory of Working Class Culture," in John Clarke et al., eds., *Working Class Culture* (London: Hutchinson, 1979), p. 214. Johnson's essay represents an early and significant attempt to use Althusser's notion of the symptomatic reading for something that Althusser would not have done, namely an historical critique. The implications of Johnson's use are extremely productive and reverb both in my historical and textual analysis (for instance, in the articulation of my conception of cultural event and in my take on dialogism).

17. Fortunately, the influence of Leavis has receded both in Williams and many others who hail from Britain. To further understand the notoriety of Leavis see Catherine Belsey, "Re-reading the Great Tradition," in Peter Widdowson, ed., *Re-Reading English* (London: Methuen, 1982), pp. 121–35.

18. Williams, *Culture and Society,* p. 289.

19. Raymond Williams, *The Long Revolution* (London: Pelican, 1965), p. 96.

20. For instance, "You see people said to me 'Arthur is a typical working man,' I said 'nonsense, he's just an individual, there're many like him perhaps but he is not a typical British working man, yet he may represent quite a lot of them. . . . ' The writer's job is to create individuals. What other people see in them as representative . . . that's their problem. My problem is to make him real and proper and then the job is finished." M.Lefranc, "Alan Sillitoe: An Interview," *Etudes Anglaises* January-March 1973, pp. 35–48. Sillitoe's point is well taken but does not quite do justice to the tales he tells. My own interest is not to ascribe typicality but specificity to his characters, a specificity that must be cognizant of the overdeterminations of class.

21. Williams, p. 288.

22. Williams, p. 311.

23. "The work of Raymond Williams, flawed as it has been by humanism and idealism, represents one of the most significant sources from which a materialist aesthetics might be derived." Terry Eagleton, *Criticism and Ideology* (London: Verso, 1976), p. 44. Eagleton, I'm sure, would be the first to admit that Williams's influence on his work was not as obvious in 1976 as it is today.

24. See, for instance, *Problems in Materialism and Culture* (London: Verso, 1980) and *The Year 2000* (New York: Pantheon, 1983). The global narrative of the latter is particularly provocative.

25. Walter Benjamin, *Illuminations* (New York: Schocken, 1969), p. 255.

26. Raymond Williams, *Culture* (London: Fontana, 1981), pp. 57–86.

27. These marks of distinction are evident in the work of Bourdieu. See chapter 1 and the bibliography.

28. Leslie Allen Paul, *Angry Young Man* (London: Faber, 1951). Should Leslie Allen Paul and Jimmy Porter have met, I'm certain they would not have got on.

29. Blake Morrison, *The Movement* (London: Methuen, 1986), pp. 10–54.

30. J. D. Scott quoted in Morrison, p. 2.

31. Quoted in Morrison, p. 3.

32. Morrison, p. 58. Morrison shows that the coherence that Davie claims was hard won and vacillated ambiguously between collective aims and individual voluntarism. Nevertheless, it is the Movement and not the socialist writing of the 1930s that prepared the cultural ground for the Angries.

33. Tom Maschler, ed., *Declaration* (New York: E. P. Dutton, 1958), pp. 7–8. Although I criticize Maschler for his public relations approach, this collection forms a very important historical document of the cultural event. For a "premature" history of the Angries see Kenneth Allsop, *The Angry Decade* (New York: British Book Centre, 1958). Subsequent page references to Maschler will be given in the text.

34. Robert Hewison, *In Anger* (London: Weidenfeld and Nicolson, 1981). This is the best cultural survey of the period under discussion despite the thin narrative on the working class contribution to the "culture of the Cold War." We might also detect a little irony in Hewison's comment on Maschler, given the title of his book.

35. Halperin, p. 182.

36. Hewison, p. 174.

37. Ingrid von Rosenberg, "Militancy, Anger and Resignation: Alternative Moods in the Working Class Novel of the 1950s and early 1960s," in Klaus, ed., p. 158. Interestingly, von Rosenberg splits the writing into two groups, political and descriptive; like Klaus, what this tends to do is emphasize the sympathetic nonworking class writers over the merely "descriptive" writing of Sillitoe et al. Despite this, von Rosenberg's research on English working-class writing puts most English academics to shame.

38. I use this term only to stress that much of what we can take to be politicization in these narratives emerges in interpersonal exchanges yet may also have macrosocial, or class, implications.

39. Walter Benjamin, "The Author as Producer," in *Reflections,* ed. Peter Demetz, trans. Edmund Jephcott (New York: Harcourt, 1978), p. 237.

40. For an explanation of these terms see chapter 1, note 33.

41. Stuart Hall, "The Rediscovery of Ideology," in *Culture Society and the Media,* ed. Michael Gurevitch et al. (New York: Methuen, 1982), p. 85. See also, Antonio Gramsci, *Selections from the Prison Notebooks,* ed. and trans. Quentin Hoare and Geoffrey Howell Smith (New York: International Publishers, 1971), especially the section, "State and Civil Society." Useful discussion of Gramsci on hegemony can also be found in Chantal Mouffe, ed., *Gramsci and Marxist Theory* (London: Routledge and Kegan Paul, 1979), pp. 168–204; Raymond Williams, *Marxism and Literature* (Oxford: Oxford University Press, 1977), and *Culture* (London: Fontana, 1981).

42. Michael Lane, *Books and Publishers: Commerce against Culture* (London: Lexington Books, 1980). Part of the problem, as Lane shows, is that many publishing jobs in England are filled through familial or old boy networks that usually center on the Oxbridge experience.

43. Quoted in Hewison, p. 141.

44. I will outline how this process dramatically altered Sillitoe's literary fortunes in chapter 5.

45. This also suggests that we need to redefine political commitment and political effec - tivity. For instance, the class effects I trace in relation to Sillitoe are hardly a copy of his own political predilections (which are diffuse but, at least in his early career, are generally leftist and specifically anarchist). Sillitoe's politics are not without their contradictions; for instance, his assertive individualism often produces support for the outsider, yet these outsiders themselves may be the source of repressive political positions. Compare, for example, these articles, "Poor People," *Anarchy* 4 (April 1964): 124–28, and "My Israel," *New Statesman* (December 20, 1974): 890–92.

## Chapter 3

1. There have been many critiques that have attempted a form of rapprochement between Marxism and deconstruction but Derrida, with his profoundly ambiguous (and rightly so) dedication to

"positioning," has never committed himself within this debate. For enthusiastic versions of Marxist deconstruction see: Michael Ryan's *Marxism and Deconstruction* (Baltimore: Johns Hopkins University Press, 1982) and Michael Sprinker's *Imaginary Relations* (New York: Verso, 1987). For an important critique of Ryan's book see John O'Kane, "Marxism, Deconstruction, and Ideology," *New German Critique* 33 (Fall 1984): 219–47. For two essays that address the problem of Bakhtin for Marxism see, Robert Young, "Back to Bakhtin," *Cultural Critique* 2 (1985–86): 71–94; and Ken Hirschkop, "Bakhtin and Democracy," *New Left Review* 160 (1986): 92–113.

2. "Post-Marxism" is a term more than a reality (in the same way that "post-capitalism" would be) but when theory has become a discourse on "hyperreality" it is small wonder that this signifier attracts so many takers, the most notable being Jean Baudrillard. The major difference between Bakhtin and Baudrillard is that the former sees sign as an arena of class struggle; for the latter sign is the successor to class struggle. Of course, there are ways that Baudrillard outlefts classical Marxism in order to reinscribe its historical urgency—but that particular argument must await a different occasion. For a general overview of the term see Richard B. Wolff and Stephen Cullenberg, "Marxism and Post-Marxism," *Social Text* 15 (Fall 1986): 126–35.

3. Peter Hitchcock, "Will the Real Mr. Bakhtin Please Stand Up?: The Polyphonic Bakhtin as a Marxist Problematic," paper delivered at the English CUNY Forum, March 1985.

4. The work of Terry Eagleton is a case in point, which includes his recent publishing project, the Rereading Literature series published by Basil Blackwell.

5. Pierre Zima, *Manuel de Sociocritique* (Paris: Picard, 1985), p. 22. In the guise of a general survey Zima here picks up on many of the themes developed in his other works—particularly in the preferences for the Frankfurt School and the "sociological" approach of Goldmann. The book also contains a useful exegesis of the work of Bakhtin, pp. 106–14.

6. V. N. Volosinov, *Marxism and the Philosophy of Language*, trans. Ladislav Matejka and I. R. Titunik (New York: Seminar Press, 1973), p. 21. Bakhtin's answer to Saussure's arbitrary sign is therefore one that is produced through social interaction and is in no way prior to that "act." For discussions of Bakhtin's critique of sign see Tony Bennett, *Formalism and Marxism* (London: Methuen, 1979), pp. 75–82; and Susan Stewart, "Bakhtin's Anti-Linguistics," in Gary Saul Morson, ed., *Bakhtin* (Chicago: University of Chicago Press, 1986), pp. 46–57.

7. See Gareth Stedman-Jones, *The Languages of Class* (Cambridge: Cambridge Universty Press, 1983). This work is discussed in more detail in chapter 1.

8. Volosinov, p. 23. Of course, Bakhtin does not mean that this arena is only evident during social crises which is why it is a working principle in my reading of Sillitoe. The point is that Bakhtin's theory allows the analysis of class struggle within and between individuals, precisely that "arena" in literary studies where class struggle has been deemed irrelevant. For a consideration of these relationships see Dominick LaCapra, *Rethinking Intellectual History* (Ithaca: Cornell University Press, 1983), pp. 291–324.

9. Mikhail Bakhtin, *Problems in Dostoevsky's Poetics*, trans. Caryl Emerson (Minneapolis: University of Minnesota Press, 1984), p. 184.

10. Mikhail Bakhtin, "Extracts from Notes (1970–1971)," trans. Vern McGee. Quoted in Gary Saul Morson, ed., *Bakhtin* (Chicago: University of Chicago Press, 1986), p. 181. See also, Tzvetan Todorov, *Mikhail Bakhtin: The Dialogical Principle*, trans. Wlad Godzich (Minneapolis: University of Minnesota Press, 1984), particularly chapters 3, 4, and 7.

11. Bakhtin does at least mention silence, but his stress on the materiality of language and its analysis through materiality precludes consideration of the ideologically repressed in language. See Morson, p. 179. For an Althusserian theorization of silence, see Pierre Macherey, *A Theory of Literary Production* (London: Routledge and Kegan Paul, 1978). An alternative but crucial feminist apprehension of silence is Tillie Olsen's *Silences* (New York: Delacourte Press, 1978). See also, Ann Rosalind Jones, "French Theories of the Feminine," in Gayle Greene and Coppelia Kahn, eds., *Making a Difference* (London: Methuen, 1985), pp. 99–101.

12. See Volosinov, pp. 65–73.

13. The breaks in the story do not suggest that "The Good Women" was written with the *Daily Worker* in mind, so analogies with Dickens's method of serialization are not relevant. The point is that I will be using Bakhtinian theory as a means of deconstructing the writer's semantic authority in relation to the dialogized language of this narrative. The serial presentation of this story throws the process of authority into relief.

14. Sign here is not a replacement for struggle but an enactment of it, as I hope to show.

15. John Berger, *Ways of Seeing* (London: Pelican, 1972), p. 7. These points are not only meant to loosen the borders of what we take to be the text, but are specifically meant to offer an interpretation of Bakhtin's theories of utterance context discussed above.

16. See Berger, chapter 3 for an early analysis of the "gaze." The page three nude continues to dominate current British tabloid papers aimed at working-class males. The *Daily Star* now offers this fare in color. The "candy floss world" that Hoggart abhorred does indeed have its reactionary elements.

17. See in particular Rosalind Coward and John Ellis, *Language and Materialism* (London: Routledge and Kegan Paul, 1977), pp. 122–52. Again, this work recalls the Althusserian debate on the role of ideology. See also, Catherine Belsey, *Critical Practice* (London: Methuen, 1980), especially chapter 2.

18. Alan Sillitoe, "The Good Women," in the *Daily Worker*, Saturday, May 24, 1962, p. 3. All further references to this version of the story will be given by date within the text.

19. Sillitoe, too, was once arrested for such protest. Apart from images of war and militarization which abound in all the forms of Sillitoe's work, there is also a consistent antinuclear theme polarized in references to the bomb. Typical of this is the poem "North Star Rocket" in Alan Sillitoe, *Sun Before Departure* (London: Grenada, 1984), p. 10.

20. See Bahktin, *Problems*, pp. 185–99. The quality of discourse here is its recognition not just of a referential object, but also someone else's speech which is dialogically figured in the utterance. The polemic that I trace in this story is articulated through a working-class purview directed at a discourse/class that opposes it.

21. Richard Hoggart, *The Uses of Literacy* (London: Chatto and Windus, 1957), p. 62.

22. Hoggart "academizes" his subject for the university set, but it is clearly tempered by a structure of feeling specific to his class origins. Sillitoe's contribution is marked by his usual appeal for identification, the use of "you" in relation to "us," although it is unclear on this occasion whether the "us" would be the reader of *Anarchy* magazine.

23. Alan Sillitoe, "Poor People," *Anarchy* 4 (April 1964): 127.

24. Sheila Rowbotham, *Woman's Consciousness, Man's World* (London: Pelican, 1973), pp.

49–66. See also Michelle Barrett and Mary McIntosh, *The Anti-Social Family* (London: Verso, 1982), pp. 59–65.

25. The passage I have in mind is where Gertrude is locked out in the garden after a violent reproach by Morel. D. H. Lawrence, *Sons and Lovers* (London: Penguin, 1976), p. 24. As for what Sillitoe thinks of Lawrence, this varies but here is an example: "I don't know. I think he's a very, very great novelist, but I hate a lot of his other trash, you know, the sort of peripheral trash which surrounded books like *The Rainbow* and *Sons and Lovers*. It was just rot and rubbish, filth and bosh, it was nothing, really." See John Halperin, "Interview with Alan Sillitoe," *Modern Fiction Studies* 25 (1979): 178. I quote this to underline that intertextuality is not just a conscious authorial appropriation but an introjection of available discourses.

26. Volosinov, pp. 87–88. Again this asserts how class struggle intersects in the individual utterance.

27. The sociological dimension of Bakhtin's theory powers both his critique of Saussure and that of the Russian Formalists. For a good introduction to the sociological dimension in Sillitoe, see Ronald D. Vaverka, *Commitment as Art* (Stockholm: Almqvist and Wiksell, 1978).

28. See Vaverka's account, p. 111.

29. Karl Miller, "Sillitoe and Son," *New Statesman* October 18, 1963, p. 530, and Mordecai Richler, "Proles on Parade," *The Spectator* October 25, 1963, p. 535.

30. Quoted in Vaverka, p. 114.

31. Volosinov, p. 86. For an analysis of these principles within the full range of Bakhtin's work see Katerina Clark and Michael Holquist, *Mikhail Bakhtin* (Cambridge: Harvard University Press, 1984), pp. 212–37. This particular chapter, however, is not without its problems, given Clark and Holquist's position on Bakhtin. Thus, in a chapter entitled "Marxism and the Philosophy of Language," Marxism is not discussed; indeed, it does not even appear as a proper noun except in the title of Bakhtin's book.

32. Volosinov, p. 13.

33. For instance, a repetition of the term "hard core" is removed in the short story collection in favor of an explanation of what the term means—in this case, the most militant protesters.

34. Alan Sillitoe, *The Ragman's Daughter* (London: W. H. Allen, 1963), pp. 173–74.

**Chapter 4**

1. Alan Sillitoe, "A Pen Was My Enemy," *Books and Bookmen* 4 (4): 11. For a brief introduction to Sillitoe's artistic development see Allen Penner, *Alan Sillitoe* (New York: Twayne Publishers, 1972).

2. For Sillitoe's account of the influence of Graves, see Alan Sillitoe, Introduction to *Saturday Night and Sunday Morning* (London: Longman, 1958), pp. vii-xii; and Alan Sillitoe, "The Long Piece," in *Mountains and Caverns* (London: W. H. Allen, 1975), p. 36.

3. Sillitoe, "Introduction," p. x. Obviously, this feeds into my interpretation of Williams's stress on the role of experience. See chapters 1 and 2.

4. Anthony West, "On the Inside Looking In," *The New Yorker* (September 5, 1959): 99–100; and Saul Maloff, "The Eccentricity of Alan Sillitoe," in *Contemporary British Novelists*, ed. Charles Shapiro (Carbondale, Ill.: Southern Illinois University Press, 1965), p. 113. For a

much more cautious evaluation see Irving Howe, "The Worker as a Young Tough," *The New Republic* 141 (August 24, 1959): 27–28. Howe contends, for instance, that there is an air of sentimentality about Sillitoe's approach that lends itself a little too easily to "current intellectual and middle class feelings about workers." As I hope my period study has shown, Howe's point is not ungrounded, yet Sillitoe is more critical of Arthur than perhaps Howe allows—as this chapter should underline.

5.  Sillitoe, "Introduction," p. xii. I am not the only one who doubts the credibility of Sillitoe's evaluation. See David Craig, "The Roots of Sillitoe's Fiction" in Jeremy Hawthorn, ed., *The British Working Class Novel in the Twentieth Century* (London: Edward Arnold, 1984), pp. 103–4.

6.  Mikhail Bakhtin, "Discourse in the Novel," in *The Dialogic Imagination*, ed. Michael Holquist, trans. Caryl Emerson and Michael Holquist (Austin: University of Texas, 1981), p. 259.

7.  Bakhtin, "Discourse," pp. 261–62. For an essay where Bakhtin links class and stylistics see V. N. Volosinov, "The Word and Its Social Function," trans. Joe Andrew in *Bakhtin School Papers*, ed. Ann Shukman (Oxford: RPT, 1983), pp. 139–52.

8.  Pierre Bourdieu, *Distinction*, trans. Richard Nice (Cambridge: Harvard University Press, 1984), p. 395.

9.  The formal problems of the novel in relation to class will be discussed in more detail in chapter 6.

10.  V. N. Volosinov, "What Is Language?," trans. Noel Owen in Shukman, p. 109.

11.  V. N. Volosinov, p. 111. This relates to my discussion of the cultural event in chapter 2 and powers the argument about the marketing of *Saturday Night and Sunday Morning* that begins the next chapter.

12.  See above, "The Long Piece."

13.  Alan Sillitoe, *Raw Material* (London: W. H. Allen, 1972). One analogy would be the career of Lawrence, whose repression of the working-class past represented by his father finally returns in the composite figure of Mellors in *Lady Chatterley's Lover*. That Sillitoe has not erased his past is evidenced by the recent *Down from the Hill* (London: Granada, 1984), a story about the road through adolescence set in Nottinghamshire and environs. For an argument that claims that Sillitoe writes best when he writes about the working-class milieu of his youth see above, David Craig, pp. 95–109.

14.  Volosinov, p. 109.

15.  Gayatri Spivak, *In Other Worlds* (New York: Methuen, 1984), p. 204. Spivak's discussion of the subaltern is an important political intervention in debates that focus on the constitution of the "Third World" subject. Here, of course, I am taking the working class as a subaltern constituency, a move with problematic implications (race and class oppressions are not variations on a theme—nor am I suggesting that), but Spivak's formulations certainly allow a loosening of the formal categorizations of class that need rethinking.

16.  Stephen Spender, "Is There No More Need to Experiment?," *The New York Times Book Review* January 26, 1964, p. 41. As both Hoggart and Worpole's studies show, this is simply not true. Part of Spender's gripe concerns his equation of working-class writing with lack of experimentation which I will also argue against. However, as a general trend in British fiction of the time there seems little reason to dispute Spender's claims. See Rubin Rabinovitz, *The Reaction*

*against Experiment in the English Novel, 1950–60* (New York: Columbia University Press, 1967).

17. Spender, p. 41.

18. Alan Sillitoe, "Proletarian Novelists," *Books and Bookmen* 4 (August, 1959): 13.

19. Sillitoe, "Proletarian," p. 13.

20. Alan Sillitoe, "Both Sides of the Street," in *The Writer's Dilemma* (London: Oxford University Press, 1961), p. 74.

21. Alan Sillitoe, *Saturday Night and Sunday Morning* (New York: Signet, 1958), pp. 7–8. This is a paperback reprint of the Alfred Knopf version of the text, although the pagination differs. The most striking feature of the Signet reprint is its sleazy cover that includes a woman in a baby-doll outfit and a man (with no legs!) sitting on pillows in an embrace. Who these characters are remains a mystery, but it is a clear that the book in the U.S. is marketed as pulp fiction—witness the blurb quoted from the *New York Times* on the cover describing the book as "a lusty, swaggering novel."

22. Ronald D. Vaverka, *Commitment as Art* (Stockholm: Almqvist and Wiksell, 1978). This is the finest full-length study of Sillitoe to date although the author's Marxist theorizing makes little use of contemporary developments in the analysis of culture emanating from France, England, or the U.S. The dependence on a theory of ideology as false consciousness is particularly debilitating in Vaverka's argument because it cannot account for the mediation of ideology through *language* in a way that apprehends both the production of hegemonic ideology and a counter-hegemonic discourse within the same work. For a recent work that discusses a range of approaches on ideology see John B. Thompson, *Studies in the Theory of Ideology* (Berkeley: University of California Press, 1984). To Thompson's discussion I would also add the name of Mikhail Bakhtin.

23. This may seem to be arguing against the grain of Lukacsian ideas on typicality. What I am trying to suggest, however, is that class subjectivity cannot be adequately addressed through the individual but rather through interaction, hence the stress on intersubjectivity.

24. The preponderance of working-class male figures, or "rogue males," in the writing of this period does not mean that the "masculine" is not problematized. Although this is more obvious in a work like Delaney's *A Taste of Honey* there are moments in Sillitoe's fiction as well—see the discussion of Liza Atkin in chapter 3.

25. For instance, "Sanity was out of reach: they were caught up in balloons of light and pleasure that would not let them go. The four acre fair became a whole world, with tents and caravans, stalls and roundabouts, booths and towers, swingboats and engines and big wheels, and a crowd that had lost all idea of time and place, locked in the belly of its infernal noise." Sillitoe, pp. 139–40. For an essay on the importance of carnival play in the English working class see Grahame Thompson, "Carnival and the Calculable," in *Formations of Pleasure* (London: Routledge and Kegan Paul, 1983), pp. 124–37.

26. For an essay that grapples with definitions of the working-class novel, see Raymond Williams, "Working Class, Proletarian, Socialist: Problems in Some Welsh Novels," in *The Socialist Novel in Britain*, ed. Gustav Klaus (Brighton: Harvester Press, 1982), pp. 110–21.

27. This does not mean that, for instance, bourgeois novelists are incapable of representing work in the novel, but that they rarely do this with the social purview of workers, even when

influenced by them. See Ruth Danon, *The Myth of Vocation* (Totowa, N.J.: Barnes and Noble, 1986).

28.   For instance, those cultural choices that constitute working-class taste could be a starting point for a more conventional content analysis of working-class fiction.

29.   Sillitoe, *Saturday*, pp. 25–26.

30.   Craig, "The Roots," p. 103.

31.   Nigel Gray, *The Silent Majority* (London: Vision Press, 1973), p. 106.

32.   See chapter 2, note 20.

33.   Two studies that take up these themes are Paul Willis, *Learning to Labour* (Farnborough: Saxon House, 1977); and Stuart Hall and Tony Jefferson, eds., *Resistance through Rituals* (London: Hutchinson, 1976).

34.   I have discussed this in relation to Sillitoe and Hoggart in chapter 2.

35.   Sillitoe, *Saturday*, p. 30.

36.   Sillitoe, *Saturday*, pp. 34–35.

37.   The relevant text here is Mikhail Bakhtin, *Problems of Dostoevsky's Poetics*, ed. and trans. Caryl Emerson (Minneapolis: University of Minnesota Press, 1984), especially chapter 5. Bakhtin's discourse schema is a little slippery at times but generally we can take double-voiced discourse to be discourse framed in the recognition of another's discourse. In parody these two voices continously wrestle for greater emphasis and is said to be vari-directional if neither voice within the utterance gains semantic authority.

38.   See chapter 2 on the postwar condition of the English working class.

39.   See David Craig and Michael Egan, "Historicist Criticism," in *Re-Reading English*, ed. Peter Widdowson (London: Methuen, 1982), pp. 208–22.

40.   Obviously, my phrasing would not fit with Craig and Egan's anti-Althusserian stance, but then my use of history is not so far removed from their position that they would not see an ally in the *use* of evidence.

41.   Sillitoe, *Saturday*, p. 175.

42.   This is probably not an adaptation of Bakhtin's theory that he would agree to: what I am suggesting is that the working-class effects of this novel counter the unifying tendencies of "literary" language. Politically, such language does not seek to renew the literary by adding yet another curious deviation, but rather threatens to abolish the literary—at least, in its predominant sense. For Bakhtin's interpretation see, *The Dialogic Imagination*, pp. 271–73.

43.   It is central not just because the episode tells us about Arthur and his relationship to women, but also because it is a fictional representation of what the social situation of the working class can mean to women in particular at a specific moment in history.

44.   Mary Eagleton and David Pierce, *Attitudes to Class in the English Novel* (London: Thames and Hudson, 1979), pp. 131–32.

45.   For examples of two by no means complimentary theoretical articulations of class and sexual politics, see Christine Delphy, *Close to Home* (Amherst: University of Massachusetts Press, 1984); and Michele Barrett, *Women's Oppression Today* (London: Verso, 1980).

46. See Mikhail Bakhtin, *Speech Genres*, eds. Caryl Emerson and Michael Holquist, trans. Vern McGee (Austin: University of Texas Press, 1986), pp. 134–35. Since this appears as part of his later work, one can assume that he was beginning to see the importance of the nonarticulated, although it is unlikely that anything more than notes is extant.

47. For instance, Irving Howe, "The Worker as a Young Tough," *The New Republic* 141 (August 24, 1959): 27–28.

48. See *The Dialogic Imagination*, pp. 3–83. Given the political connotation that the novel has engendered as form there seems to be a need for further clarification on the process of novelization that Bakhtin describes.

49. Williams, "Proletarian," p. 111.

**Chapter 5**

1. The importance of a working-class readership cannot be overestimated. While it is true that there is a large amount of bourgeois writing that is not read by the middle class—indeed it is specifically targeted at the working class—the suggestion here is that class cultural intervention must involve the working class both as producers *and* as consumers. Whether or not the middle class reads pulp fiction does not threaten its relative dominance in the sphere of culture, but this is precisely the case when the working class itself establishes an alternative cultural interest.

2. Obviously, although this definition maintains that all working-class fiction should be popular, not all popular fiction will be working-class. Worpole's readership analyis is an excellent critique of the British book industry. See Ken Worpole, *Reading by Numbers* (London: Comedia, 1984).

3. It would become one of the first British million-seller books in paperback. By 1975 its total sales in England and the U.S. were 2.7 million copies—not bad for a book that W. H. Allen had merely "taken a chance" on. Figures quoted from Ingrid von Rosenberg, "Militancy, Anger and Resignation," in *The Socialist Novel in Britain*, ed. Gustav Klaus (Brighton: Harvester Press, 1982), p. 142.

4. John Halperin, "Interview with Alan Sillitoe," *Modern Fiction Studies* 25 (1979): 177.

5. See Richard Hoggart, *The Uses of Literacy* (Harmondsworth: Penguin, 1958). For an extremely interesting account of working-class reading habits from a worker's perspective, see Peggy Temple, "Experience of Literacy in Working Class Life" in *The Politics of Literacy*, ed. Martin Hoyles (London: Writers and Readers, 1977), pp. 79–85.

6. Halperin, p. 177.

7. See chapter 1, note 30.

8. The draped jacket is often associated with the Teddy boys, whose parody in dress of well-to-do Edwardians has made them one of the more researched English working-class subcultures. See, for instance, Dick Hebdige, *Subculture: The Meaning of Style* (London: Methuen, 1979). Personally, I find Arthur's suits in the film more reminiscent of the Mods, but he does not fit that description in any other way.

9. See the notes to Jeffrey Richards and Anthony Aldgate, *British Cinema and Society, 1930–1970* (Totowa, N.J.: Barnes and Noble, 1983).

10. For an important analysis of *Coronation Street,* see Richard Dyer et al., eds., *Coronation Street* (London: British Film Institute, 1981). The series still runs on TV, although it does not bear the air of nostalgia about community that accompanied its introduction. Nineteen sixty also sees the introduction of Dr. Martens boots, the staple footwear of working-class youth well into the 1970s. Recently, the shoes have become a fashion item—see Desson Howe, "Prescriptions for the Sole," *The Washington Post,* Sunday, January 11, 1987, Section F.

11. Lindsay Anderson, "Get Out and Push," in *Declaration,* ed Tom Maschler (London: E. P. Dutton, 1958), pp. 140–41.

12. The list includes *Saturday Night and Sunday Morning, Look Back in Anger, A Taste of Honey, The Loneliness of the Long Distance Runner, This Sporting Life,* and *A Kind of Loving.* Note, it is interesting that these films achieved a remarkable popularity when cinema attendance in England was in a general decline (with the advent of TV). Given that most of them were also the product of an independent film company, Woodfall, their success is even more remarkable, although, as was shown in chapter 2, this event is not without explanation.

13. For an overview of the Free Cinema and Woodfall projects in which Anderson, Richardson, and Reisz were prominent see Roy Armes, *A Critical History of the British Cinema* (New York: Oxford University Press, 1978), pp. 263–79.

14. See Robert Stam, *Reflexivity in Film and Literature* (Ann Arbor: UMI Research Press, 1985). Stam is one of the first critics to attempt to explore the implications of Bakhtinian theory for the study of film. It is also evident in Gilles Deleuze's discussion of Pasolini in Gilles Deleuze, *Cinema 1. The Movement-Image,* trans. Hugh Tomlinson and Barbara Habberjam (Minneapolis: University of Minnesota Press, 1986), pp. 72–76. My own use will be much more in the spirit of Bakhtin's dialogism even when using Genette's terminology.

15. This "direct" approach has its theoretical problems, but the important point is that Free Cinema managed to challenge some widely held misconceptions about working-class life, in spite of the class prejudice of its major proponents.

16. Armes, p. 264. The lack of self-analysis will be crucial to the botched ending of *Saturday Night and Sunday Morning* as we will see.

17. Richard Hoggart, "We Are the Lambeth Boys," *Sight and Sound* 28 (Summer–Autumn 1959): 164–65. Hoggart, in true self-deprecating fashion, writes this "review" as a letter—perhaps to underline his major point about Reisz's "subjective" approach. What is interesting is that Reisz's first feature film seems a partial response to Hoggart's criticisms. Reisz, indeed, appears to want to address the "more demanding (and more exciting) problems of the imagination."

18. Alan Sillitoe, "What Comes on Monday," *New Left Review* 4 (July–August 1960): 58–59.

19. Quoted in Alexander Walker, *Hollywood, U.K.* (New York: Stein and Day, 1974), p. 38.

20. Two early examples of this position are Alan Sillitoe, "Arthur Seaton Is Not Just a 'Symbol,'" *Daily Worker* (January 28, 1961): 2; and Thomas Wiseman, "Everybody Got Me Wrong, Says Mr. Sillitoe," *Evening Standard* (September 1, 1961): 8. Sillitoe's main complaint is not with symbols (after all, he names Arthur Seaton using his own initials), but with labels which he believes codify him and his work in damaging ways. Sillitoe's resistance to class analysis has always been strong in interviews, even those in leftist journals, but is rarely apparent in the fiction itself, a point explored by David Craig, "The Roots of Sillitoe's Fiction," in *The British Working Class Novel in the Twentieth Century,* ed. Jeremy Hawthorn (London: Edward Arnold, 1984), pp. 95–110.

21. Walker, p. 82.

22. See Richards and Aldgate, chapter 10 for a full discussion of the journey of *Saturday Night and Sunday Morning* through the *BBFC*. Sillitoe has complained more than once about the censorship that his script underwent even, as we will see, at the hands of Karel Reisz.

23. Mikhail Bakhtin, *Problems of Dostoevsky's Poetics*, ed. and trans. Caryl Emerson (Minneapolis: University of Minnesota Press, 1984), pp. 79–85. For instance, "a monologic artistic world does not recognize someone else's thought, someone else's idea, as an object of representation." In our context, this means that the middle-class censors cannot "recognize" the language of their working-class "Other."

24. This issue is obviously larger than our immediate concerns, but see, for instance, Stephen Heath's discussion of narrative space for an indication of film's problematic relation to "reality." *Questions of Cinema* (Bloomington: Indiana University Press, 1981), chapter 2.

25. The part of the palette that seems to interest Richardson is grey, which dominates the flashback scenes of life in the Smith household. Technically, Richardson was a stronger director than Reisz, but what the latter may have lacked in technique he more than made up for in empathy, which is almost completely lacking in Richardson's camera style in his Sillitoe film.

26. Robboe's coat is not pure white, but it still stands in direct contrast to Arthur's work clothes. For Eisenstein's comments on black and white see Sergei Eisenstein, *The Film Sense*, ed. and trans. Jay Leyda (New York: Harcourt, Brace, Jovanovich, 1970), chapter 3.

27. Colin MacCabe, *Tracking the Signifier* (Minneapolis: University of Minnesota Press, 1985), p. 35.

28. MacCabe, p. 37.

29. Quoted in Georg Gaston, *Karel Reisz* (Boston: Twayne Publishers, 1980), p. 33.

30. Quoted in David Craig, *The Real Foundations* (London: Chatto and Windus, 1973), pp. 282–83.

31. John Russell Taylor, *Masterworks of the British Cinema* (New York: Harper and Row, 1974), pp. 267–68. Although this purports to be a script of the film, there are many differences with the text that reached the screen. I have thus used my own notes or, on this occasion, Sillitoe's own recollections of the soliloquies for the film. See Alan Sillitoe, "What Comes on Monday," p. 58.

32. Russell Taylor, p. 268.

33. For an essay that looks at the way positive images of the working class are sacrificed for older stereotypic formulas of both class and masculinity, see John Hill, "Working Class Realism and Sexual Reaction," in *British Cinema History*, eds. James Curran and Vincent Porter (Totowa, N.J.: Barnes and Noble, 1983), pp. 303–11.

34. Gaston, p. 34.

35. For a pertinent discussion of Godard, see Brian Henderson, "Toward a Non-Bourgeois Camera Style," in *Movies and Methods*, ed. Bill Nichols (Berkeley: University of California, 1976), pp. 422–37.

36. Karel Reisz, *The Technique of Film Editing* (London: Focal Press, 1953), p. 28.

37. Sillitoe, "What Comes on Monday," p. 59.

**Chapter 6**

1. As the most popular form of fiction writing, the novel is the most contestable cultural terrain. To this extent, the attention that it has received from those interested in the possibilities of the working-class novel seems justified. For discussion of such issues see Jeremy Hawthorn's preface to *The British Working Class Novel in the Twentieth Century,* ed. Jeremy Hawthorn (London: Edward Arnold, 1984), pp. vii-x; Raymond Williams, "Working Class, Proletarian, Socialist," in *The Socialist Novel,* ed. Gustav Klaus (Brighton: Harvester Press, 1982), pp. 110–21; Carole Snee, "Working Class Literature or Proletarian Writing?" in *Culture and Crisis in Britain in the Thirties,* eds. John Clark et al. (London: Lawrence and Wishart, 1979) and "Walter Brierley: A Test Case," *Red Letters* 3 (1976); Roy Johnson, "Walter Brierley: Proletarian Writing," *Red Letters* 2 (1976); and Roy Johnson, "The Proletarian Novel," *Literature and History* 2 (1975). Sillitoe, despite the label, has also written on the proletarian novel, "Proletarian Novelists," *Books and Bookmen* 4 (August 1959): 13. He describes his first encounter with Tressell's *The Ragged Trousered Philanthropists* which showed Sillitoe that the life he had led was "interesting enough to be written about." Tressell also proved to Sillitoe that such writing could be artistically shaped in the novel.

2. Bernstein constructs a hermeneutics of the practice of novel-writing by establishing that the novel is "essentially" Kantian in form—a point developed through his reading of Lukacs's *Theory of the Novel.* The reason Bernstein's argument often seems convoluted is because he is treating the novel as a theoretical problem within the history of philosophy, in contrast to, for instance, Ian Watt's empirical analysis within the history of literature. J. M. Bernstein, *The Philosophy of the Novel* (Minneapolis: University of Minnesota Press, 1984).

3. See Bruce Robbins, *The Servant's Hand* (New York: Columbia University Press, 1986).

4. John Berger, *The Sense of Sight* (New York: Pantheon, 1985), p. 15. For an analysis of Berger's form of storytelling, see Bruce Robbins, "Feeling Global: John Berger and Experience," in *Postmodernism and Politics,* ed. Jonathan Arac (Minneapolis: University of Minnesota Press, 1986), pp. 145–61.

5. Berger, p. 14.

6. See Michael Pickering and Kevin Robins, "The Making of a Working-Class Writer," in Hawthorn, p. 140.

7. Walter Benjamin, "The Storyteller," in *Illuminations,* ed. Hannah Arendt, trans. Harry Zohn (New York: Schocken, 1969), p. 84. My sense is that Benjamin's essay can be employed as an answer, or complementary critique to Bernstein's philosophy of the novel for the notion of "aura," Benjamin's veritable tradition-building principle, is bound up in a collective art of storytelling that does not sit easily with the individualist subjectivism that marks the novel.

8. Chief among these is, of course, "The Loneliness of the Long Distance Runner." As chapter 3 shows, my own preference is for "The Good Women." The idea here is that the short story is not hampered by the exigencies of plot development endemic to the novel. To this degree, and perhaps to this degree only, the short stories are more like the vignettes and slice-of-life tales redolent in the mind of the storyteller.

9. David Craig, "The Roots of Sillitoe's Fiction," in Hawthorn, p. 98. The book in question is *The Storyteller* (London: W. H. Allen, 1979).

10. Alan Sillitoe, *Raw Material* (London: W. H. Allen, 1972), pp. 149–50. This book contains some of Sillitoe's strangest writing, but also some of his most powerful polemic. The last sections, for instance, oscillate between rabid prescriptions about the duty of the writer and brilliant commentary on the state of the nation. Although Sillitoe revised the book in 1974 its major premises and confusions remain "intact."

11. There are many examples of the Lukacsian approach, the finest being Frederic Jameson's *Marxism and Form* (Princeton: Princeton University Press, 1971) and *The Political Unconscious* (Ithaca: Cornell Univ. Press, 1981). Recently, Jameson has been extending his critical methods to "Third World" literature, and not entirely successfully. See, "Third World Literature in the Era of Multinational Capitalism," *Social Text* 15 (1986): 65–88.

12. Paul Willis and Philip Corrigan, "Orders of Experience," *Social Text* 7 (1983): 85–103. This essay is not only a good overview of the English debate on "discourse" in the late 1970s, but a working paper on some of the more salient aspects of British culturalism.

13. Alan Sillitoe, "The Good Women," in *The Ragman's Daughter* (London: W. H. Allen, 1963).

14. See Ken Worpole, "Expressionism and Working Class Fiction," in *Dockers and Detectives* (London: Verso, 1983), pp. 77–93; and Tony Davies, "Unfinished Business: Realism and Working Class Writing" in Hawthorn, pp. 125–36.

15. This period is dealt with in more detail in chapter 1.

16. See Catherine Belsey, *Critical Practice* (London: Methuen, 1980), especially chapters 3 and 4. Of course, this is the very realism that Lukacs defended with such verve, particularly against the aesthetic inclinations of modernism.

17. The gesture here is toward a theoretical exploration of the possibilities for an interrogative realist text in a period where modernism is not only questioned, but dismissed.

18. Jean Baudrillard, *In the Shadow of the Silent Majorities*, trans. Paul Foss et al. (New York: Semiotexte, 1983). To be fair to Baudrillard, this denigration should be read within the context of a failure of "vision" in the French Left. See, for instance, Jean Baudrillard, *La Gauche Divine* (Paris: Bernard Grasset, 1985).

19. Here I am drawing from the work of Ernest Mandel, *Late Capitalism,* trans. Joris De Bres (London: Verso, 1978), p. 393. Mandel claims that Britain had one of the few, if not the only, working classes that did not suffer a major setback during the thirty-year period up to the mid-sixties (economically). But this relative stability at the economic level was nevertheless being undermined at the cultural level, as is shown both by the staging of Sillitoe's fiction and by the content of some of the stories themselves.

20. Frederic Jameson, "Postmodernism, or the Cultural Logic of Late Capitalism," *New Left Review* 146 (July-August 1984): 56. For a response that both questions and complements Jameson's argument, see Terry Eagleton, "Capitalism, Modernism and Postmodernism," *New Left Review* 152 (July-August 1985): 60–73. The point here is not to dismiss Jameson out of hand, for he does seem to have touched upon the major cultural processes of our present time. The challenge is to see whether his theory allows any space for oppositional culture that is class-based but not postmodern according to his definitions.

21. Raymond Williams, *Marxism and Literature* (Oxford: Oxford University Press, 1977), p. 123.

22. See above Worpole, *Dockers.*

23. Davies, p. 135.

24. Williams, p. 124.

25. See above Williams, chapter 9; and *The Long Revolution* (London: Pelican, 1965), pp. 64–88. Although the latter is the more lucid account, the essay in *Marxism and Literature* is more theoretically productive, charged as it is with Williams's reading of Gramsci's work on hegemony—which provides precisely the historical understanding of cultural apparatus that makes "structures" of feeling significant in any sense. There are still problems, of course, not the least of which is that Williams's conception of "feeling" itself may be based on an organic community to which Williams can no longer appeal (at least, not in the sense discussed in *The Long Revolution*).

26. Williams, *Marxism*, pp. 133–35.

27. Alan Sillitoe, *The Loneliness of the Long Distance Runner* (London: W. H. Allen, 1959), pp. 12–13. Although this story has not been discussed in great detail in this work, Smith's tale is in many ways indicative of the central tenets of my "reading." For instance, Smith speaks as a rebel who is as individually defined as any Sillitoe character, but the claims that are expressed in the quoted passage cannot simply be explained in terms of individualist critique. Whenever Sillitoe uses phrases like "blokes like me" one knows instinctively that there are several voices at work in such an utterance, including that of class. That such positions are unstable and inconsistent should not deter the critic from attempting to understand the voices spoken, or the audiences addressed. There are many other voices besides those being spoken through Smith, but they need to be heard. Bakhtin once said that he heard voices in everything; for this particular critic that means hearing the dialogism of the oppressed.

# Bibliography

Allen, Walter. "In the World of the Bottom Dogs." *The New York Times Book Review* (March 25, 1962): 5.

———. "The Newest Voice in English Lit Is from the Working Class." *The New York Times Book Review* (December 20, 1959): 4.

Allsop, Kenneth. "I Starved for *Saturday Night and Sunday Morning*." *Daily Mail* (February 16, 1961): 10.

———. "Sillitoe Rings the Bell." *Daily Mail* (December 29, 1959): 4.

———. *The Angry Decade*. New York: British Book Centre, 1958.

Althusser, Louis. *Lenin and Philosophy and Other Essays*. London: New Left Books, 1971.

———, and Etienne Balibar. *Reading Capital*. London: New Left Books, 1970.

Anderson, Perry. *Arguments within English Marxism*. London: Verso, 1980.

———. *In the Tracks of Historical Materialism*. London: Verso, 1983.

Arac, Jonathan, ed. *Postmodernism and Politics*. Minneapolis: University of Minnesota Press, 1986.

Armes, Roy. *A Critical History of the British Cinema*. New York: Oxford University Press, 1978.

Aronowitz, Stanley. *The Crisis in Historical Materialism*. New York: Praeger, 1981.

Atherton, Stanley S. "Alan Sillitoe's Battleground." *Dalhousie Review* 48 (1968): 324–31.

Bakhtin, M. M. *The Dialogic Imagination*. Edited by Michael Holquist. Translated by Caryl Emerson and Michael Holquist. Austin: University of Texas Press, 1981.

———. *Problems of Dostoevsky's Poetics*. Translated by Caryl Emerson. Minneapolis: University of Minnesota Press, 1984.

———. *Speech Genres*. Edited by Caryl Emerson and Michael Holquist. Translated by Vern McGee. Austin: University of Texas Press, 1986.

Baro, Gene. "A New, Impressive Talent." *New York Herald Tribune Book Review* (August 16, 1959): 6.

———. "Tales of British Working Class Life." *New York Herald Tribune Book Review* (May 29, 1960): 6.

Bell, Daniel. *The End of Ideology*. New York: Harper and Row, 1962.

Belsey, Catherine. *Critical Practice*. London: Methuen, 1980.

Benjamin, Walter. *Illuminations*. Edited by Hannah Arendt. Translated by Harry Zohn. New York: Schocken, 1969.

———. *Reflections*. Edited by Peter Demetz. Translated by Edmund Jephcott. New York: Harcourt Brace, Jovanovich, 1978.

Berger, John. *The Sense of Sight*. New York: Pantheon, 1985.

———. *Ways of Seeing*. London: Pelican, 1972.

Bernstein, Basil. *Class, Codes and Control*. Vol 1. London: Routledge and Kegan Paul, 1971.

Bernstein, J. M. *The Philosophy of the Novel*. Minneapolis: University of Minnesota Press, 1984.

Blackwell, Trevor, and Seabrook, Jeremy. *A World Still to Win.* London: Faber, 1985.

Bourdieu, Pierre. *Distinction.* Translated by Richard Nice. Cambridge: Harvard University Press, 1984.

————. *Outline of a Theory of Practice.* Translated by Richard Nice. New York: Columbia University Press, 1977.

Boyd, Ronald E. "A Critical Introduction to the Proletarian Novels of Alan Sillitoe." Unpublished M.A. thesis: North Texas State University, 1969.

Clark, John et al., eds. *Culture and Crisis in the Thirties.* London: Lawrence and Wishart, 1979.

Clark, Katerina, and Holquist, Michael. *Mikhail Bakhtin.* Cambridge: Harvard University Press, 1984.

Clarke, John et al., eds. *Working Class Culture.* London: Hutchinson, 1979.

Coleman, John. "The Unthinkables." *New Statesman* (October 27, 1961): 610, 612.

Craig, David. "The British Working Class Novel Today." *Zeitschrift für Anglistik und Amerikanistik* 11 (1963): 29–41.

————, ed. *Marxists on Literature: An Anthology.* Harmondsworth: Penguin, 1975.

————. *The Real Foundations.* London: Chatto and Windus, 1973.

Curran, James, and Porter, Vincent, eds. *British Cinema History.* Totowa, N.J.: Barnes and Noble, 1983.

Curtis, Jean-Louis. "Une Furieuse Solitude." *La Nouvelle Revue Française* 148 (April 1965): 709–12.

Danon, Ruth. *The Myth of Vocation.* Totowa, N.J.: Barnes and Noble, 1986.

Denny, N. "The Achievement of the Long-Distance Runner." *Theoria* 24 (1965): 1–12.

Denning, Michael. *Mechanic Accents.* London: Verso, 1987.

Eagleton, Mary, and Pierce, David. *Attitudes to Class in the English Novel.* London: Thames and Hudson, 1979.

Eagleton, Terry. *Criticism and Ideology.* London: Verso, 1976.

————. *The Function of Criticism.* London: Verso, 1984.

————. *Literary Theory.* Minneapolis: University of Minnesota Press, 1983.

————. *Marxism and Literary Criticism.* Oxford: Oxford University Press, 1976.

————. *Walter Benjamin: Or Toward a Revolutionary Criticism.* London: Verso, 1981.

Eisenstein, Segei. *Film Sense.* Edited and translated by Jay Leyda. New York: Harcourt, Brace, Jovanovich, 1970.

Elloway, David. Introduction to Keith Waterhouse/Alan Sillitoe, *Billy Liar/The Loneliness of the Long-Distance Runner.* London: Longman, 1971, pp. 201–28.

Foster, Hal, ed. *The Anti-Aesthetic.* Port Townsend: Bay Press, 1983.

Foster, John. "The Declassing of Language." *New Left Review* 151 (1985): 29–45.

Gaston, George. *Karel Reisz.* Boston: Twayne Publishers, 1980.

Gindin, James. "Alan Sillitoe's Jungle," in *Postwar British Fiction.* Berkeley: University of California Press, 1962, pp. 14–33.

Gramsci, Antonio. *Selections from the Prison Notebooks.* Edited and translated by Quentin Hoare and Geoffrey Howell Smith. New York: International Publishers, 1971.

Gray, Nigel. *The Silent Majority: A Study of the Working Class in Post-War British Fiction.* London: Vision Press, 1973.

Gurevitch, Michael et al. *Culture Society and the Media.* New York: Methuen, 1982.

Hajek, Igor. "Morning Coffee with Sillitoe." *The Nation* (January 27, 1969): 122–24.

Hall, John. "What the Hell's Class?" *The Guardian* (March 24, 1970): 8.

Halperin, John. "Interview with Alan Sillitoe." *Modern Fiction Studies* 25 (1979): 183.

Hawthorn, Jeremy, ed. *The British Working Class Novel in the Twentieth Century.* London: Edward Arnold, 1984.

Hebdige, Dick. *Subculture: The Meaning of Style.* London: Methuen, 1979.

Hewison, Robert. *In Anger.* London: Weidenfield and Nicolson, 1981.

Hirschkop, Ken. "Bakhtin and Democracy." *New Left Review* 160 (1986): 92–113.

Hoggart, Richard. *The Uses of Literacy.* Harmondsworth: Penguin, 1958.

Howe, Irving. "In Fear of Thinking." *The New Republic* (May 28, 1962): 25–26.

――――. "The Worker as a Young Tough." *The New Republic* (August 24, 1959): 27–28.

Hoyles, Martin, ed. *The Politics of Literacy.* London: Writers and Readers, 1977.

Hurrell, John Dennis. "Alan Sillitoe and the Serious Novel." *Critique* 4 (Fall-Winter, 1960–1961): 3–16.

Hutt, Allen. *The Post-War History of the British Working Class.* London: Victor Gollancz, 1937.

Jameson, Frederic. *Marxism and Form.* Princeton: Princeton University Press, 1971.

――――. *The Political Unconscious.* Ithaca: Cornell University Press, 1981.

――――. "Postmodernism or the Cultural Logic of Late Capitalism." *New Left Review* 146 (July-August 1984): 53–92.

Johnson, Richard. "What Is Cultural Studies Anyway?" *Social Text* 16 (Winter 1986/7): 38–80.

Johnson, Roy. "The Proletarian Novel." *Literature and History* 2 (1975).

Keating, P. J. *The Working Classes in Victorian Fiction.* London: Allen and Unwin, 1971.

Kettle, Arnold. "Alan Sillitoe Opens a Door." *Daily Worker* (October 16, 1961): 2.

――――. "The Artist and Politics." *Marxism Today* (May 1959): 139–45.

Klaus, H. Gustav. *The Literature of Labour.* New York: St. Martin's Press, 1985.

――――. *The Socialist Novel in Britain.* Brighton: Harvester Press, 1982.

Laclau, Ernesto. *Politics and Ideology in Marxist Theory.* London: New Left Books, 1977.

Lane, Michael. *Books and Publishers: Commerce against Culture.* London: Lexington Books, 1980.

Lentricchia, Frank. *Criticism and Social Change.* Chicago: University of Chicago Press, 1983.

Lefranc, M. "Alan Sillitoe: An Interview." *Etudes Anglaises* (January-March 1973): 35–48.

Lukacs, George. *Essays on Realism.* London: Lawrence and Wishart, 1980.

――――. *History and Class Consciousness.* London: Merlin Press, 1971.

――――. *The Theory of the Novel.* London: Merlin Press, 1971.

Lyotard, Jean-Francois. *The Postmodern Condition.* Translated by Geoff Bennington and Brian Massumi. Minneapolis: University of Minnesota Press, 1984.

MacCabe, Colin. *Tracking the Signifier.* Minneapolis: University of Minnesota Press, 1985.

Macherey, Pierre. *A Theory of Literary Production.* London: Routledge Kegan Paul, 1978.

Maloff, Saul. "The Eccentricity of Alan Sillitoe." In *Contemporary British Novelists.* Edited by Charles Shapiro. Carbondale: Southern Illinois University Press, 1965, pp. 95–113.

Mandel, Ernest. *Late Capitalism.* London: Verso, 1978.

Marwick, Arthur. *British Society since 1945.* London: Pelican, 1982.

Marx, Karl. *Grundrisse.* Translated by Martin Nicolaus. New York: Vintage, 1972.

――――, and Engels, Friedrich. *The German Ideology.* London: Lawrence and Wishart, 1963.

Maschler, Tom. *Declaration.* New York: E. P. Dutton, 1958.

Matveyeva, Nina. "Alan Sillitoe Visits Our Office." *Soviet Literature* 9 (1963): 180–82.

McDowell, Frederick P. W. "Self and Society: Alan Sillitoe's *Key to the Door.*" *Critique* 6 (Spring 1963): 116–23.

Moody, Philippa. "In the Lavatory of the Athenaeum: Post-War English Novels." *Melbourne Critical Review* 6 (1963): 83–92.

Morrison, Blake. *The Movement.* London: Methuen, 1986.

Morson, Gary Saul, ed. *Bakhtin.* Chicago: University of Chicago Press, 1986.

Mouffe, Chantal, ed. *Gramsci and Marxist Theory.* London: Routledge and Kegan Paul, 1979.

Mudrick, Marvin. "Man Alive." *The Hudson Review* 17 (Spring 1964): 117–18.

Nagel, Wolfgang. "Gesprach mit Alan Sillitoe." *Merkur* 29 (August 1975): 760–72.

Nardella, Anna Ryan. "The Existential Dilemmas of Alan Sillitoe's Working Class Heroes." *Studies in the Novel* 5 (Winter 1973): 469–82.

O'Flinn, Paul. *Them and Us in Literature.* London: Pluto Press, 1975.

Penner, Alan R. *Alan Sillitoe.* New York: Twayne Publishers, 1972.

Pritchett, V. S. "Saints and Rogues." *The Listener* (December 6, 1962): 957–59.

Rabinovitz, Rubin. *The Reaction against Experiment in the English Novel, 1950–1960.* New York: Columbia University Press, 1967.

Richards, Jeffrey, and Aldgate, Anthony. *British Cinema and Society 1930–1970.* Totowa, N.J.: Barnes and Noble, 1983.

Raven, Simon. "Two Kinds of Jungle." *The Spectator* (October 20, 1961): 551.

Reisz, Karel. *The Technique of Film Editing.* London: Focal Press, 1953.

Richler, Mordecai. "Proles on Parade." *The Spectator* (October 25, 1963): 535.

Robbins, Bruce. *The Servant's Hand.* New York: Columbia University Press, 1986.

Rosenberg, Ingrid Von. *Der Weg nach oben: englische Arbeiterromane 1945–78.* Frankfurt: Grossen Linden, 1980.

Roskies, D. M. "Alan Sillitoe's Anti-Pastoral." *Journal of Narrative Technique* 10 (1980): 170–85.

Rowbotham, Sheila. *Hidden from History.* London: Pluto, 1973.

Russell Taylor, John. *Masterworks of the British Cinema.* New York: Harper and Row, 1974.

Shestakov, Dmitri. "Alan Sillitoe from Nottingham." *Soviet Literature* 9 (1963): 176–79.

Shukman, Ann, ed. *Bakhtin School Papers.* Oxford: Russian Poetics in Translation, 1983.

Shutz-Guth, Gudrun, and Schutz, Helmut. *Typen des britischen Arbeiterromans.* Frankfurt: Grossen Linden, 1979.

Sillitoe, Alan. Selected works:

**Fiction:**

_____. *Saturday Night and Sunday Morning.* London: W. H. Allen, 1958.

_____. *The Loneliness of the Long Distance Runner.* London: W. H. Allen, 1959.

_____. *The General.* London: W. H. Allen, 1960.

_____. *Key to the Door.* London: W. H. Allen, 1961.

_____. *The Ragman's Daughter.* London: W. H. Allen, 1963.

_____. *Guzman, Go Home.* London: Macmillan, 1968.

_____. *Travels in Nihilon.* London: W. H. Allen, 1971.

_____. *Men, Women and Children.* London: W. H. Allen, 1973.

_____. *The Widower's Son.* London: W. H. Allen, 1976.

_____. *The Storyteller.* London: W. H. Allen, 1979.

_____. *The Second Chance and Other Stories.* London: Jonathan Cape, 1981.

_____. *Her Victory.* London: Granada, 1982.

_____. *The Lost Flying Boat.* London: Granada, 1983.

_____. *Down from the Hill.* London: Granada, 1984.

_____. *Life Goes On.* London: Granada, 1985.

_____. *Out of the Whirlpool.* London: Hutchinson, 1987.

**Poetry:**

_____. *The Rats and Other Poems.* London: W. H. Allen, 1960.

_____. *Sun Before Departure.* London: Granada, 1984.

**Essays and Articles:**

_____. "The Pen Was My Enemy." *Books and Bookmen* (January 1959): 11.

_____. "Proletarian Novelists." *Books and Bookmen* (August 1959): 13.

_____. "What Comes on Monday." *New Left Review* 4 (July-August 1960): 58–59.

_____. "Both Sides of the Street." *The Writer's Dilemma.* London: Oxford University Press, 1961, pp. 68–75.

————— . "Arthur Seaton Is Not Just a 'Symbol.'" *Daily Worker* (January 28, 1961): 2.

————— . "Novel or Play?" *The Twentieth Century* (February 1961): 206–11.

————— . "Symbolism Must Merge with Realism." *Books and Bookmen* (October 1961): 7–8.

————— . *Road to Volgograd.* London: Macmillan, 1964.

————— . "Drilling and Burring." *The Spectator* (January 3, 1964): 11–12.

————— . "Poor People." *Anarchy* 4 (April 1964): 124–128.

————— . "The Wild Horse." *The Twentieth Century* (Winter 1964/5): 90–92.

————— . Introduction to Robert Tressell, *The Ragged Trousered Philanthropists.* London: Panther, 1965, pp. 7–10.

————— . Introduction to *A Sillitoe Selection.* Edited by Michael Marland. London: Longman, 1968, pp. 125–33.

————— . *Raw Material.* London: W. H. Allen, 1972.

————— . "My Israel." *New Statesman* (December 20, 1974): 890–92.

————— . *Mountains and Caverns.* London: W. H. Allen, 1975.

Sinfield, Alan, ed. *Society and Literature.* London: Methuen, 1983.

Smith, Bruce Michael. "Looking Back at Anger." *DAI* 42 (1981): 4203A (Indiana University).

Spark, Muriel. "Borstal Boy." *The Observer* (October 11, 1959): 21.

Spender, Stephen. "Is There No More Need to Experiment?" *The New York Times Book Review* (January 26, 1964): 41

Spivak, Gayatri Chakravorty. *In Other Worlds.* New York: Methuen, 1987.

Stam, Robert. *Reflexivity in Film and Literature.* Ann Arbor: UMI Research Press, 1985.

Staples, Hugh B. *"Saturday Night and Sunday Morning:* Alan Sillitoe and the White Goddess." *Modern Fiction Studies* 10 (Summer 1964): 171–81.

Stedman-Jones, Gareth. *The Languages of Class.* Cambridge: Cambridge University Press, 1983.

Stephane, Nelly. "Alan Sillitoe." *Europe* 417–418 (1964): 289–93.

Thompson, E. P. *The Making of the English Working Class.* New York: Vintage, 1966.

————— . *The Poverty of Theory and Other Essays.* New York: Monthly Review Press, 1978.

Thompson, Grahame. "Carnival and the Calculable." In *Formations of Pleasure.* London: Routledge and Kegan Paul, 1983.

Thompson, John B. *Studies in the Theory of Ideology.* Berkeley: University of California Press, 1984.

Updike, John. "Voices from Downtroddendom." *The New Republic* 142 (May 9, 1960): 11–12.

Vaverka, Ronald Dee. *Commitment as Art.* Stockholm: Almqvist and Wiksell, 1978.

Vicinus, Martha. *The Industrial Muse.* London: Croom Helm, 1973.

Volosinov, V. N. *Marxism and the Philosophy of Language.* Translated by Ladislav Matejka and I. R. Titunik. New York: Seminar Press, 1973.

Wain, John. "Possible Worlds." *The Observer* (October 12, 1958): 20.

Walker, Alexander. *Hollywood, U.K.* New York: Stein and Day, 1974.

West, Anthony. "On the Inside Looking In." *The New Yorker* (September 5, 1959): 99–100.

Widdowson, Peter. *Re-Reading English.* London: Methuen, 1982.

Williams, Raymond. *Culture and Society.* London: Chatto and Windus, 1958.

————— . *Culture.* London: Fontana, 1981.

————— . *The Long Revolution.* London: Pelican, 1965.

————— . *Marxism and Literature.* Oxford: Oxford University Press, 1977.

————— . *Problems in Materialism and Culture.* London: Verso, 1980.

————— . *Writing in Society.* London: Verso, 1983.

Willis, Paul, and Corrigan, Philip. "Orders of Experience." *Social Text* 7 (1983): 85–103.

Wilson, Keith. "Arthur Seaton Twenty Years On." *English Studies in Canada* 7 (December 1981): 414–26.

Wood, Ramsay. "Alan Sillitoe: The Image Shedding the Author." *Four Quarters* 21 (November 1971): 3–10.
Worpole, Ken. *Dockers and Detectives*. London: Verso, 1983.
———. *Reading by Numbers*. London: Comedia, 1984.
Zima, Pierre. *Manuel de Sociocritique*. Paris: Picard, 1985.

# Index